Copyright Elliot George 2014

All rights reserved.

No part of this publication may be reproduced,
or transmitted, in any form or by any means,
electronic, mechanical, photocopying, recording
or otherwise, without prior permission in writing
from the publisher.

Published by Ideasun Ltd
Spike Lodge, The Street, East Preston,
LITTLEHAMPTON, West Sussex, BN16 1JL
United Kingdom of Great Britain

Ideasun Limited.
Reg. No. 4021004
Registered office:
Martlet House, Unit E1, Yeoman Gate, Yeoman Way,
Worthing, BN13 3QZ, United Kingdom of Great Britain

Godbuster
Exorcises all known gods

By **Elliot George** (copyright 2014)

Acknowledgements
Many thanks to my proofreaders, particularly James W Cox and Pastor A Nonymous

"*It is far better to grasp the Universe as it really is than to persist in delusion, however satisfying and reassuring.*

§

If we long to believe that the stars rise and set for us, that we are the reason there is a Universe, does science do us a disservice in deflating our conceits?

§

We have also arranged things so that almost no one understands Science and Technology. This is a prescription for disaster. We might get away with it for a while, but sooner or later this combustible mixture of ignorance and power is going to blow up in our faces"

Carl Sagan

FOREWORD

I think a good personal reason for abandoning Christianity would be to rebel against Yahweh for allowing, no *demanding* child sacrifices, slavery and the denigration of women and homosexuals, *and* for rejecting freedom of conscience and freedom of speech. All of this goes against the First Amendment of the American Constitution. My moral intuitions are such that I refuse to worship a God so barbaric. Many other religions are little better. The objective evidence for the truth of a faith would need to be overpoweringly convincing to overcome these personal moral intuitions of mine.

I have defended this line of reasoning on my blog, "Debunking Christianity." Just go there and do a search for "There Isn't a Bad Reason to Reject the Christian Faith."

http://debunkingchristianity.blogspot.com/search/label/argument%20from%20ignorance]

Now, along comes Elliot George with this excellent book. George shows us there are many good logical, scientific and objective reasons to reject all religions. So on the one hand there aren't any bad personal reasons to reject Christianity and on the other hand there are many good logical, scientific and objective reasons not to have faith in any faith.

So, if my argument that there isn't a bad personal reason to reject Christianity isn't convincing to you, then George's book should be. If, however, my argument is convincing, then taken *together* with George's book, Christianity and all religions will be revealed as intellectually bankrupt with no value at all in the marketplace of ideas. If there really is a divine CEO, he should be jailed for incompetence and gross deception.

In either case, I highly recommend this book. It's a small one but it packs a big punch: small but mighty. It's inexpensive enough to hand out to family and friends too, so do it.

John W. Loftus, ex-preacher and author of "Why I Rejected Christianity" and "The Outsider Test for Faith."

CONTENTS

	Page
Introduction	9
Chapter 1. Why do we Believe?	13
Chapter 2. Belief in Perspective	27
Chapter 3. Does Belief have Value?	41
Chapter 4. Evidence.	53
Chapter 5. What is Science?	69
Chapter 6. The Quest for Truth.	75
Chapter 7. Origin of the Universe	83
Chapter 8. Evolution.	95
Chapter 9. Morality and Forgiveness.	123
Chapter 10. Sin, Heaven and Hell.	133
Chapter 11. The Case against Religion.	139
Chapter 12. Living without 'God'.	163
Raison d'être	173
Afterthought	177
Some Unholy Questions	178
Postscript	179

"I don't believe in Science. Science is our defence against belief."
Harvard Professor of Psychiatry, J. Allan Hobson
Is the Prof a traitor?
Read on to find out...

Introduction

I'm a retired Science teacher who believes it is of paramount importance to improve the public understanding of Science. It is especially necessary to get journalists and priests to be more knowledgeable because they are in a position to promote and act upon dangerous misinformation.

If journalists recognised the difference between correlation and causality, unvaccinated children in Wales might not be suffering from measles right now. If priests knew the importance of vaccination, polio might have been eliminated from its last pockets of infection in Nigeria. In both of these cases, children are suffering because of ignorance of Science.

Religions have been fighting a rearguard action against the acceptance of Science ever since Scientific Method was introduced. Embarrassingly for religious leaders, scientific discoveries keep revealing that the ancient scriptures are not reliable sources of knowledge; this is why those leaders have to employ faith to defend their institutions. People of strong faith often have misunderstandings about what Science is and how it works. As this book tries to explain, once they have been through the process, scientific facts do not require believing although they are provisional and forever open to the possibility of revision.

Believers tend to seek material that reinforces their desire for certainty and to avoid material that expresses opposite opinions. Belief gets locked up in a strongbox inside the believer's head.

No, Science does not have all the answers. Only a fool would claim that, no proper scientist would. Sadly, the lack of a complete set of knowledge enables believers to point to things like love and beauty and crow, *"Science can't explain poetry! What about that?"* Well, no, not yet anyway, although the latest neuro-imaging techniques enable researchers to witness the birth of an idea so I wouldn't rule out further developments.

That desire for total black or white certainty is in our minds; we abhor doubt. The fact is that perfect resolution of all our questions is unobtainable, but that doesn't mean that a non-evidential god (a god that is merely an idea unsupported by evidence) is the answer. Science definitely has the best method for investigating and understanding everything around us.

And no, Science is not perfect. For a start it *proves* nothing; it only provides levels of probability. Secondly, to the consternation of seekers of certainty, it sometimes produces *and accepts* new evidence that requires the modification of previously held positions. Thirdly, scientists are human and so there are a few rogues, but the fact that they are often exposed and dealt with shows a willingness on the part of scientists to present a respectable and honourable discipline.

I'm sorry if most of my examples appear to target Christianity; I really wish to address all religions equally: a pox on all your houses! The apparent focus is because of an accident of birth – my own schooling was Christian therefore I know most about that faith and, since Christianity is the largest religion, it is, in my terms, the biggest problem! However, two other religions are also based on the Old Testament of the Bible: Judaism and Islam; taken together they encompass most of mankind.

Godbuster challenges believers to open their eyes to Scientific Reality – a worldview based on evidence. This will not be easy. Science is a *culture*; a whole way of thinking which is different from non-scientific thought. It requires unusual levels of questioning, scepticism, investigation and objectivity, together with a preparedness to accept the evidence even if it contradicts your preconceptions. Just believing what you have been told is a much easier option.

Never forget that the Afar natives of Ethiopia believe that baboons were once people who, having displeased god, were punished by being banished into the wilderness. When you think, *"That is ridiculous and plain ignorant!"* just remember that they, or people in the future, are equally entitled to think that what *you* believe is ridiculous and plain ignorant.

Please note, I am not against the moderately religious; many good people are believers. Nor am I against god; that would be foolish because she is, currently, a non-evidential proposition. I am against religion. I don't want to ban it; I want to discredit it with education, as has already happened to many thousands of beliefs.

I do not seriously expect this book to convert diehard believers, nothing could do that, but I do hope that it will provide reassurance to doubters that they are not abnormal. Let's abandon confirmation bias and reclaim the word *'belief'* to mean *'things we aren't really sure about'*!

■■

"Nothing is known with absolute certainty. We have to learn how to handle doubt and uncertainty."
Physicist Richard Feynman

1. WHY DO WE BELIEVE?

Simple – we have become adapted to believe. We have a 'god-shaped hole' in our brains. It's a side effect of our evolution to survive the challenges of the environment.

Early humans who ate a poisonous plant without recognising the relationship between its consumption and their subsequent illness, ate it again and suffered again, possibly fatally. Even rats, seeing a number of dead rats around a fast-acting poisoned bait, learn to avoid it.

The people who learned that effects usually have a cause, and who deliberately avoided the hazards they had discovered, lived longer and therefore had greater opportunity to pass on their genes to more offspring. By virtue of their reasoning and knowledge these people were better adapted to parent *more* children: that's survival of the fittest in action. Naturally they taught their children about the dangers and to look out for 'cause and effect' so that their family could be more successful. Consequently, the proposition that 'effects have a cause' conferred an evolutionary advantage and became accepted as a 'truth'. *Was it the very first human belief?*

So, humans have evolved 'an ability', that is the brain 'hardware and software', for recognising the connection between cause and effect, for holding the belief that cause precedes event. This means that the very concept of 'believing' is transmitted from generation to generation by both nature and nurture. The tendency is passed down in our genes and is reinforced by parenting; we're on the look out for things to 'believe' from the day we're born!

If we learn a belief in infancy it seems to be absorbed deep into our psyche – it becomes more like an instinct than a memory and therefore is difficult to erase later in life. This propensity enabled a speedy reaction to risks for primitive man in the wild, it made sense then to *indelibly* learn about the hazards early in life, but it causes problems in the form of 'righteous' certainty and fundamentalism in the modern world. *Is there a blurred boundary between an instinct and a belief acquired in infancy?*

Over the past few thousand years, we have modified our environment so rapidly that we have exceeded our physical bodies' ability to adapt to the changing conditions. One example of this concerns our eyes; they are perfectly good for the distant vision needed in the open expanses where we first evolved but, now that we use them to closely scrutinise text, they soon require the assistance of spectacles. *No such restriction applies to thinking, are we now evolving in our heads and, therefore, in our societies?*

Richard Dawkins coined the word 'memes' for these ideas that are transmitted from person to person down the generations. They are often beneficial to our species (I'm not ruling out the possibility that other species may also have 'learned beliefs').

Such beliefs as *'cause precedes effect'* can be life saving. Arguably the human species wouldn't have become so numerous and conquered so many habitats without them. No wonder our brains have become adapted to recognise *connections;* to discover patterns; to find causes. No wonder we think our beliefs are important. *Should we now ask whether we have gone overboard and bolstered the value of beliefs to an undeserved level?*

It's fine to assign high value to *supported* beliefs; ones based on evidence but, the brain's searching for causes often interacts with another tendency that we have evolved: *persistence* in the application of our 'programming'. For example, all animals that care for their young have developed the ability to visually recognise faces (and, to a lesser extent, other familiar objects); it helps if offspring can identify their parents and vice versa! This is a highly developed skill that we persist in using even where it may be inappropriate. We imagine we can see a man's face on the moon, animals in the clouds or Jesus' face in a tortilla. It's a phenomenon known as 'pareidolia'.

In the same way as we persist in applying our facial recognition skills, inappropriately, to clouds in the sky, so we may also persist in trying to find a cause where there may be none, to creating 'beliefs' where there is no supporting evidence. There is no brake on false beliefs unless the scrutiny of logic is engaged.

Raising such speculation to the level of a 'belief' is where religions come into the picture. Since this sort of belief is not supported by evidence, religious leaders have found it necessary to counter the inevitable difficult questions by claiming immunity from questioning! In that way they have managed to suppress rival opinions. They have even managed to elevate *unquestioning* to a position of virtue and 'righteousness' in our societies by calling it 'Faith'!

"To learn who rules over you, simply find out who you are not allowed to criticize."
Voltaire

Non-evidential beliefs are simply follies; they are beliefs beyond justification. Before we assign them any value, we should examine how important these beliefs really are: take a Reality Check. Scientists would call those speculative beliefs 'hypotheses' and would construct investigations to test their validity.

Seeking causality can be expressed as asking the question 'why'? It is a difficult question to answer compared to 'who?', 'when?', 'what?', 'which?' and 'where?' and it may not always be a valid question to ask because it often presumes there is a cause where there may be none. Some things happen by pure chance; it's not appropriate to ask, *'why did that tossed coin land heads up?'* There is no causal answer.

Nevertheless, the expectation of causality makes us feel a need to find reasons for our experiences and, by extension, a purpose for our lives, an explanation for our existence and an explanation for the origin of the universe. It is probably the reason why man is a curious animal and it is the motivation behind exploration and scientific investigation.

Our brains, being adapted to investigate the problem of what caused the effects we encounter, will keep looking for connections and, if none is forthcoming we feel unfulfilled. This leads to a need for solutions and for certainties. Doubt is uncomfortable; it leaves us still searching vainly for a cause, for a purpose. The 'certainty' of belief (even if non-evidential) is comforting. *Shouldn't we beware of falling into its clutches?*

When we are looking for the ultimate cause, *how do we know when we've got there? How do we know when to stop searching?* It can only be by choice. It might be an informed choice supported by evidence, in which case it will not require believing or, it might be a subjective opinion based on nothing more than personal preference, like the decision to add sugar to coffee; in that case, belief becomes just a fickle bet.

The business of searching for causes usually doesn't end with the first solution. An effect is often only the first link in a chain so finding the first cause merely prompts another question, another *'why?'* This is the start of a chase with a storyline that has a beginning, a middle and, hopefully, an end. It resonates with the human life experience which begins with birth, continues through life and ends in death; no wonder we feel a kinship with narrative.

The activity of following a narrative trail to a fruitful conclusion harks back to man's hunter-gatherer days – the mode of life we originally evolved to fulfil. Our niche in our habitat is that of top predator; we are usually the pursuers, not often the pursued.

Hunting is a rewarding experience, providing satisfaction in the capture and entertaining thrills along the way. Our tendency to persist in a search or hunt explains why we enjoy puzzles and why we feel good when we follow a sequence and achieve a solution. Endorphins, such as serotonin and dopamine, flood our brains, stimulating our pleasure centres.

Since the development of language and campfire storytelling we have been able to enjoy the same pleasures in virtual form. Now that mankind has invented writing and other media, we can enjoy narratives that have been recorded in various ways: books, audio, video, and they may be available in a broadcast or online form; we are in the post Gutenberg printing press period: the information age.

Our predilection for narrative explains the attention we give to stories, and their popularity. Music also rewardingly employs our analytical minds, especially when it ends with a resolution – the dominant seventh followed by the tonic chord.

Does this also explain why many of us don't like movies which lack a proper ending? You know, that feeling you get when you leave a cinema unfulfilled and disappointed instead of uplifted. Maybe, since there was no resolution, no 'capture', no endorphin was released and its non-appearance leaves us still searching for a conclusion and feeling dissatisfied...

Brains that are adapted for such involvement are uncomfortable when they are idle – our desire to persist in analysis is frustrated and we feel bored. A lack of input to our brains may actually be damaging; sensory deprivation can be used as a torture and there is some recent evidence to indicate that people who lack the challenge of stimulation in their lives are more likely to succumb to Alzheimer's disease.

So, the desire to exercise the functionality of the brain explains why we are driven to continue to seek the comfort of answers, of solutions, of certainty. Many of us even embark upon puzzles with delight. Does this explain our fascination with mystical things like ghosts, zombies, vampires, spirits and the Loch Ness monster? Such activity has given us analytical minds, powerful thinking capability which adopts the assumption that there must be a solution, an *absolute truth*. In the absence of such a result, the temptation is to invent one; hence the popularity of religions and conspiracy theories.

Let's consider the lives of our pet cats. Our relationship with cats over the millennia has resulted in an evolution of their behaviour. They have learned that they don't have to become snarling adults hunting for prey. In the domestic environment they now retain their kittenish personality throughout life. It's a role that suits humans looking for a pet to care for. *Have we made them a feline 'heaven on Earth'?*

Biologists call this retention of juvenile behaviour 'Infantilism'. From the cat's point of view, a cat owner is a god-like protector and provider of security, of *certainty*. The cat enjoys a highly desirable life of idleness and luxury. *Could it be that inventing a 'caring father in the sky' is a human attempt at self-infantilism? Do we WANT a god?*

It certainly suits some church leaders to keep their flock in juvenile mode. Liberal Christian Bishop, John Shelby Spong says, *"The church is in the guilt and control business. It doesn't like the people to grow up, because you can't control grown-ups. That's why we talk about being 'born again'. If you're 'born again', you're still a child."*

Did the authors of the 'Holy Scriptures' understand that we prefer to live life in Faith, Hope and Trust and that we enjoy stories? Did they, unconsciously or consciously, create their religions to meet our psychological requirements? Is that why they have provided us with parables and myths?

Human Optimism

Optimism is another trait that we have evolved. We can't live a useful life without hope of future progress. We like to hope that our fellow men are good, that we will live forever and that our beliefs are true. This is 'The Audacity of Hope' that President Barack Obama wrote about. Loss of hope, *hopelessness*, causes people to lose self esteem, become depressed, cease to function properly and, in acute cases, to self harm, submit to abuse or commit suicide.

We have to imagine we are invincible and immortal or we will sink into depression. Most of us fear death so an optimistic belief in an 'afterlife' is an insurance policy against death. It's an attractive idea, a reason to deny the finality of death. Many of us will resist any attempt to come to terms with the likely reality: that death is the end, so we attempt to deny any information that disagrees with our personal bias.

We prefer to believe our own denial and convince ourselves that our beliefs are true by using the word 'Faith'. Once we have achieved the 'Faith' state of mind, nothing anyone can say will convince us otherwise. We literally believe our religion as though our lives depend on it. Our 'afterlives' *do* depend on it! Denial rules! We're a funny bunch!

> *"You can't reason a man out of something he wasn't reasoned into."*
> **Jonathan Swift**

The desire for an afterlife also plays into the hands of the authors of 'holy scriptures' and they have duly provided the desired goods. There are many different types of afterlife – each religion has come up with its own version: Jews have seven heavens (they are a hierarchy from the entry level to the most sublime, hence the expression, 'to be in seventh heaven'), Muslims have Paradise, Buddhists have Nirvana, Nordic Pagans had Valhalla, etc. (See Chapter 9)

So, if those are the reasons why people believe in a god, what are the reasons for them to join a religion? Some motives are personal and some are social, I suspect.

We all feel good, get a smug glow of self satisfaction when we think we are being virtuous and 'righteous'. Church attendance can provide that sanctimonious feeling (as can membership of a political party), and there is a benefit to belonging to an organisation – we are herd animals. The notion of there being a 'caring father in the sky' is undoubtedly comforting, as is the prospect of an afterlife. Certainty is also comforting and religions purport to provide answers to the 'questions of life' such as how and why we are here.

The social reasons are about connections. Before we alienate our family, friends and workmates by adopting different views, which they may interpret as implying that they are stupid, much 'soul' searching needs to be undertaken. There is a lot of lifestyle to lose.

Summary

Our brains are adapted to:
- Find causes for the effects we observe; to investigate why?

- Persist in the attempt to interpret observations in terms of previously encountered experiences or knowledge even if inappropriate.

- Enjoy following a trail, or its virtual equivalent, a tale.

- Seek an end; an 'absolute truth'.

- Be satisfied with a happy ending (a proper conclusion to a narrative or solution to a puzzle).

- Dislike idleness – brains prefer to be active.

- Prefer certainty to doubt.

- Imagine we are indestructible – it won't happen to us. Hopefully!

Taken together, the above qualities explain why we enjoy seeking to understand and to solve puzzles, particularly the biggest puzzle of all: the world around us. That is the impetus behind exploration and scientific investigation.

Human brains have evolved to seek an answer to the question *"What is the meaning of Life, the Universe and Everything?"* (with thanks to Douglas Adams) and, frustratingly, although we now know more than ever before thanks to Scientific Method, there's always been insufficient evidence to provide a perfect and complete answer. *So, what's the easiest solution?* Invent a god.

That's why every human society has done just that; there have been many thousands of gods, most of them have been discredited already but a few remain, hence the need for this book. The current batch of gods is not special; many of them share characteristics with extinct ones; some surviving gods are newish and some are older but not exceptionally so – belief in some Ancient Egyptian gods lasted for many thousands of years.

Conclusion

Human brains have evolved to embark on a 'Quest for Truth' (see chapter 6). We have a 'god-shaped hole'. Incidentally, this yearning for solutions correlates with the desire for reconciliation that has evolved into standards of decent behaviour for social animals like us. (See later)

Celebrity Quotes

"Religion arose from the uniquely human need for causal explanations."
Lewis Wolpert CBE FRS FRSL
§
"Religion is regarded by the common people as true, by the wise as false, and by the rulers as useful."
Edward Gibbon
Author of 'The History of the Decline and Fall of the Roman Empire'
§
"It is always better to have no ideas than false ones; to believe nothing than to believe what is wrong"
Thomas Jefferson
§
"The way to see by faith is to shut the eye of reason."
Benjamin Franklin

2. BELIEF IN PERSPECTIVE

What is Belief?
'A belief is a psychological state in which an individual holds a proposition or premise to be true.'
The Stanford Encyclopaedia of Philosophy

Propositions and premises are ideas inside people's heads. In many fields of endeavour, such concepts may be considered to have two levels of status: 'humble ideas' and 'grand beliefs', or equivalent words in the appropriate specialist terminology.

Science acknowledges both levels; in science a humble proposition or premise is called a hypothesis – it is an educated guess and forms the starting point for an investigation. The highest rank is known as a Scientific Theory; to qualify for that status an idea has to be supported by evidence and a consensus of expert opinion which accepts the evidence as convincing. It also has to provide predictions which can be tested for veracity.

Even then a Scientific Theory can be shown to be false if new observations do not fit the model. ('Model' in Science means a description of a phenomenon that fits the observations.) Scientific facts are *always* open to review so they are only as good as the current evidence. Tradition and popularity are no safeguards: Newton's Laws of Motion are widely accepted and served perfectly well as a gravitational model for over two hundred years until Einstein came up with his Theory of Relativity.

Despite the above caveat, the uncertainties of Science are much more secure than the 'certainties' of religions. The difference is, scientists admit their doubts, while the position of most leaders of religions is to deny doubt and dogmatically assert 'faith'.

Religions have a lower level also, in the form of 'theological concepts' such as 'limbo' (see later) but they focus on what may be regarded as the top ranking level for a concept in their field: 'beliefs'. A religious belief appears to be an idea that has been elevated in importance without supporting evidence, to be granted the status of *true* for no reason! I wouldn't go with belief or faith: it's so indiscriminating. *Why should we give 'belief' a free pass straight to the top concept level of religions? Shouldn't we demand justification?*

Believers seem to recognise that the lack of supporting evidence for their propositions makes them vulnerable to disbelief because they feel the need to express their doctrines (ideas) *dogmatically*. Dogma is the repeated, arrogant, stubborn assertion of opinion as though it is fact. It is no credible substitute for evidence, and the enlisting of it by religions should be a clue to their weakness, their lack of foundation. Worse than that, believers put their beliefs in a strong box in their heads and secure it with the padlock of 'faith'. We must guard against dogma and 'faith'; together they outlaw freethinking and compel conformity and submission.

A Scientific Theory is *not* equivalent to a religious belief. Scientific Theories are models of reality supported by evidence. Since the evidence comes in the form of repeatable observations of phenomena *outside* of men's heads, they can be rediscovered by anyone, anywhere and any time. This means that scientific facts do not require belief, they supersede it.

On the other hand, religious ideas (doctrines) are merely ideas *inside* men's heads, just opinions, often *ancient* opinions instigated in a time of profound ignorance when men thought the Sun went round the Earth.

"The existence of god is not subjective. He either exists or he doesn't. It's not a matter of opinion. You can have your own opinion but you can't have your own facts."
Ricky Gervais

Unfortunately, in ordinary language, a 'theory' means a 'guess' thereby causing much misunderstanding! Semantics has a lot to answer for!

How do we get into the 'psychological state' of believing?
There are five main ways:

<u>By Authority</u>
This usually happens as a result of following an adult's example when we are young. Parents don't realise how much influence they have even when they are not trying to exert any – my two-year-old daughter wanted to shave after watching me! We should be very careful about how we act in front of children. Humans are apes (members of the order Primates) and we learn by aping; our children are little apes.

Some 'authorities' don't deserve devoted respect: in the year 2000, 'Infallible' Pope John Paul II admitted the RC church had been wrong to imprison Galileo 300 years earlier. The Church of England has just apologised for its treatment of Darwin.

<u>By Revelation</u>
'Born again' George W Bush claimed god told him to invade Iraq and Afghanistan; if he'd said he had received the message through his hairdryer we would

have locked him up as insane! (Thanks to Sam Harris for that line.)

Some people claim to experience a vision or hear the voice of god. Well, brains are very fragile organs; they can be induced to hallucinate by exercise, drugs, dreams, hyperthermia, flashes of light, blindness, sensory deprivation, magnetic pulses, meditation, illness, migraines or blows on the head. See the following website for how easily your brain can be deceived:

http://www.wadsworth.com/psychology_d/templates/stripped_features/try_online/tryonline.html

<u>By Tradition</u>

This is based on the notion that lots of people have held the particular belief for a very long time and they can't all be wrong. Well, check out the following:

The Ancient Egyptians believed in their gods for 6000 years before the birth of Christ. Their beliefs are dead now – *weren't they wrong?*

The natives of Papua New Guinea, practiced cannibalism right up until the second half of the twentieth century. They thought they were helping their loved ones travel to the next world by consuming their bodies! Human brains were considered particularly delicious apparently. Sadly, the practice transmitted the prion disease Kuru; many went mad and died early. *Weren't they wrong?*

The Aztecs believed that, if they didn't sacrifice a human and hold up his, still beating, heart to the setting sun, it wouldn't rise next morning. *Weren't they wrong?*

Even leaders can make mistakes, as pointed out above 'infallible' Pope John Paul II admitted the Catholic Church had been wrong about Galileo. The electorate are no better - in the nineteen thirties, millions voted for Hitler. *Weren't they all wrong?*

Popularity and durability are not evidence of correctness. Please remember, an idea does not gain truth as it gains followers.

"To err is human."
Alexander Pope

But popularity does indicate the *size of support* for the ideas of a religion in the same way that the vote in an election indicates the size of support for the policies of a political party. Do you want to vote for religious atrocities?

By Indoctrination

Young Christians in the Bible belt of the USA are put under peer pressure to conform; this happens in many sects. Some charismatic leaders have been able to indoctrinate their followers to such an extent that they have voluntarily committed group suicide. Sadly, it seems that some people are unusually vulnerable to suggestion.

See: http://en.wikipedia.org/wiki/Cult_suicide

In some religions active attempts are made to radicalise young men into the doctrines (the ideas of the religion). Some extremist Muslims are persuaded to become suicide bombers and promised 72 virgins in 'Paradise' upon their 'martyrdom'!

By Choice

Some countries make it compulsory for babies to be inducted into the state religion shortly after birth: *there is no choice for them!* Since we are born without names or religious labels, it is merely a question of which believer gets to us first and that's still largely a matter of geography.

Very few of us actively choose to change our beliefs and those who do predominantly choose non-belief. The population of the USA that self-identify as atheist has increased by 400% in the past five years! At that rate it will be 25% by 2018 and 100% by 2022!

Are you a chooser?

Many claim that they *reaffirmed* their commitment to their parents' religion when they were old enough to make an informed choice. Seventy percent of us retain the same religion as our parents. It's not even our *own* choice! *Isn't that abdicating choice to a senior power?*

Did you REALLY have a free choice?

I know someone who says he didn't know he was a Muslim until he saw what the officials had put in his passport! For the bureaucrats and, *therefore for him*, the location of his birth was of paramount importance while his personal 'belief', whatever that was, was not.

Do you call yourself a Christian? There are about 41,000 different Christian denominations; *did you really survey the whole field and select the most appropriate sect for you?*

Could you have become a Jain if you had really wanted to? Do you know what the Baha'i religion entails? Did you consider worshipping Ixcacao, the Mayan goddess of chocolate? What about Cloacina, the Roman goddess of sewers? Can you really claim to have a full working knowledge of all the beliefs there have ever been and to have chosen the most appropriate one for you? Did you really make a fully informed decision?

Did the Pope Choose?
Were his parents Catholic by any chance? What would he be now if he had been born in Iran? An Ayatollah? Yes, you may draw a beard and turban on his picture!

Is your religion just an accident based on the location of your birth and the faith of your parents?

How important is choice?
Remember, *choosing* is how we decide lots of things, such as which horse to back in the Grand National and how much sugar to put in our coffee. *How important are these personal preferences?*

Don't forget, if you've chosen something, you can *'unchoose'* it: I went off sugar thirty years ago. Millions have given up smoking cigarettes. Doesn't this mean that, since we can be fickle and change them when we feel like it, our choices are trivial – *they can't be very important, can they?*

Men change their beliefs all the time – Cassius Clay gave up Christianity for Islam and had to change his name to Mohammed Ali; Tony Blair changed from protestant to Catholic; a friend of mine was raised as a member of the Plymouth Brethren and is now an Evangelical Christian. Many men undergo a 'deathbed' conversion. *Surely, such changes indicate how insignificant our personal beliefs are, don't they?*

On the other hand, scientific facts do not require believing, they are supported by evidence, which can be discovered and rediscovered by anyone, anywhere, at any time. Religious beliefs have no such foundation; they are, at best, merely personal choices and, like a preference for dark chocolate as opposed to milk chocolate, are monumentally unimportant.

Of course, choices can inspire actions and it would be foolish to argue that actions are unimportant. The choice of security, which stimulated the construction of the Great Wall of China, for example, obviously created an important monument! Sadly, the actions inspired or excused by religious choices are far more detrimental than they are beneficial.

Summary

We:

    Often abdicate the selection of our religious denomination to our parents.
    Usually become inducted into the prevalent local religion in the area where we are born.

Can change our minds about which is the 'true god'; the ability to simply *'unchoose'* and change religion surely undermines the claims of religions to have exclusive possession of certainty and 'righteousness'. Some religious societies enforce capital punishment for 'apostasy' in an attempt to prevent such wilful changes.

Surely, the fact that mankind has many different religions, and has had many thousands more in the past that are now defunct, makes it unlikely that any of them can meet the claim to be the 'correct' one, the 'righteous' one, the only path to 'heaven'. *Doesn't it?*

Conclusion
Imagining that *your* beliefs, *your* ideas, *your* opinions, *your* choices are important is the height of arrogant conceit. *Isn't it?*

"There are, in fact, two things, Science and opinion; the former begets knowledge, the latter ignorance."
Hippocrates

A Hierarchy of Information Credibility

1. Absolute 'Truth' – only available as a concept.
2. Proven facts – only available in mathematics – concepts such as the square on the hypotenuse is equal to the sum of the squares on the other two sides of a triangle.
3. Scientific Theories and Laws of Physics: models of reality that fit observations and enable predictions that can be investigated to validate the propositions, and which have not been falsified yet. They have a high probability of being correct but are *not* regarded as having been *proved* beyond all doubt.
4. Scientific Facts supported by a consensus of expert agreement on the convincing nature of evidence in the form of repeatable observations.
5. Data from investigations in progress, observations newly discovered – no expert consensus yet, but directions for further research may be indicated.
6. Corroborated Records or Remains: historical evidence or inference from two or more separate sources.
7. Hypotheses: educated guesses that are the starting points for investigations.
8. Speculations: unsubstantiated ideas that purport to answer questions and may give rise to superstitions, religions, myths and fantasies or conspiracy theories.

The eight levels of credibility of information range from 1= highest credibility, to 8 = lowest credibility. See later chapters for explanations of truth, proof and evidence.

The following are subjective reactions by humans to propositions at any level of credibility; they are decisions made inside men's heads:

a) Beliefs: support that can be attached to any proposition however incredible. Belief has nothing to do with truth. You can believe a rope bridge will take your weight but when it snaps you will have a couple of seconds of falling to realise that belief was not true!

b) Faith: a system of strongly held but unfounded beliefs. Confidence is not faith. It is a calculation of statistical probability based upon best estimates of sources of error. Trust is not faith. It is the level of reliability of a source or proposition based on previous experience.

c) Doctrines: ideas purporting to be answers or principles, which are repeatedly asserted as though they are facts, often identified as dogma.

To those who say that Scientific Theories such as Evolution and Relativity require faith, I say, no they don't – they have statistical probability instead.

"It doesn't matter how beautiful your theory is, it doesn't matter how smart you are. If it doesn't agree with experiment, it's wrong.

*

The first principle is that you must not fool yourself and you are the easiest person to fool"

Richard Feynman

***

"Religion has convinced people that there's an invisible man ... living in the sky. Who watches everything you do every minute of every day. And the invisible man has a list of ten specific things he doesn't want you to do. And if you do any of these things, he will send you to a special place, of burning and fire and smoke and torture and anguish for you to live forever, and suffer, and suffer, and burn, and scream, until the end of time. But he loves you. He loves you.
He loves you, and he needs money!"

George Carlin

3. DOES BELIEF HAVE VALUE?

Scientific Facts have no use for it

Scientific facts simply do not require belief. Information which has been discovered by repeatable observations can be rediscovered by anyone, anywhere, at any time. Scientific facts are not just beliefs, not just propositions, not just ideas inside men's heads; they are discoveries of the properties of external phenomena. If everyone died today and a new humanoid species evolved they would be able to rediscover Science exactly as we know it now. No doubt they would also invent religions, probably starting with sun worship because it's such an iconic object, but it is extremely unlikely they would come up with the exact same story about a carpenter's son who could walk on water and got crucified.

As an example of the redundancy of belief for evidential facts, gravity has obeyed the same rules since the beginning of the Universe, billions of years before men evolved, and will continue to obey the same rules after mankind becomes extinct. *There is no danger of gravity disappearing if we cease to 'believe' in it, is there!* It's true that our *understanding* of gravity has changed from the Newtonian model to the Einsteinian model as more observations have come in.

Scientists understand that all knowledge is provisional and that it's acceptable to change their minds.

> *"If the evidence shows I am wrong, I will change my mind. Changing your mind when the evidence changes is a sign of intelligence"*
> **Professor Edzard Ernst**

'Scientists understand that it's acceptable to change their minds.' Just think what that means: *scientific facts are not fixed and 'true' forever.* They are simply the best *current* understanding of reality. If new evidence comes in, the model may have to be revised. Scientists are prepared to listen to opposing opinions; they do not claim to have perfect answers or even to be able to provide proof, *only probability.*

How unlike the unbending culture prevalent in most faith based organisations! Believers tend to make unfounded assertions, stifle opposition and try to strengthen their doctrine by unceasing repetition. *Do you think they have to dogmatically protect their doctrine because they perceive that the lack of supporting evidence makes it vulnerable to dissent?*

Let's put the lie to an often heard accusation – that Science or atheism is a religion and its proponents are its believers. I don't think so! *Scientific facts do not require belief*. They are in the environment waiting to be discovered, again and again if necessary. They were there before men ever walked on the Earth and there is no reason to think that they will cease to exist when our species has died out – they have survived the extinction of 90% of species after all.

Unlike a religion, which is a shared belief, atheists (non-believers) have nothing to share. We don't need to have a communal attitude towards all the things that have no evidence for existence, such as Santa Claus and the tooth fairy. If we did, that would be a full time job! Think about it - if non-belief is a religion then baldness is a hairstyle, and **not** cycling is a hobby!

Scientific protocols are designed with the intention of eliminating the subjective element of men's brains, and therefore any bias, from the business of gathering observations. That's why it insists on replicability – one person may have got a fluke result but that would be unlikely to happen to others. It doesn't always succeed in this goal, but *it is a commendable aim, isn't it?*

Unfortunately, bias can still be inserted in the interpretation of evidence. It's difficult to separate men's subjectivity and personal ambitions from the whole process, that's why there is a stage called 'Peer Review' in which rival scientists have the opportunity to point out weaknesses in the methodology of the investigation which produced the conclusions that are being claimed. This self-policing mechanism attempts to root out spurious claims and ensure the praiseworthy reputation of scientific information.

Incidentally, Newton's gravitation model is not *wrong*. It is accurate enough for us to send spacecraft to flyby the moons of Neptune. Only when we are considering locations close to the sun, outside the Solar System or velocities close to the speed of light, do we need to invoke the slightly greater accuracy of Einstein's Theory of Relativity.

Some scientific facts are supported by such convincing evidence that they are accepted as *highly* probable and therefore are unlikely to be challenged. In these cases, the consensus of agreement has extended beyond the community of expert Science specialists into the general population. For example, few would seriously dispute Galileo's description of the Earth orbiting the Sun now.

So should we keep the word 'belief' for things we are uncertain about?
Things such as, "I believe Tom is hiding in the bedroom". That's how I think it should be used, *what do you think?*

There are plenty of uncertainties to form beliefs about, including questions at the frontiers of scientific investigation such as the Origin of the Universe: experts debate which hypothesis to support. When new data arrives which confirms one alternative or another, the answer becomes a known fact and belief is no longer required.

Yes, facts that have the support of convincing evidence and a consensus of expert agreement do not need believing. In that situation, the word 'belief' is redundant and the status of the information as merely being 'a proposition or premise', an idea in men's heads, is dropped.

Religions do not meet the criteria required for factualness. Religious 'answers' to the 'questions of life' are not supported by evidence; they are merely hypotheses; that's why they need the support of 'faith'.

Is belief important then?
Stone Age men probably had beliefs – *were they important?* We don't know much about their culture but it seems likely that they worshipped the animal prey that they depicted on their cave walls or prayed to a god for a successful hunt. *Were their beliefs important?*

4500 yrs ago, in the Bronze Age, Egyptians believed in Horus who was regarded as a sky god – his right eye was supposed to be the sun and his left eye the moon! *Was that belief important?*

3500 yrs ago, in the early Iron Age, the Indo-Persians believed in Mithras who was born out of a rock – an event that was celebrated on December 25th. He performed miracles such as getting water out of rocks! *Was that belief important?*

3000 yrs ago, the Ancient Romans believed in Dionysus who was born of a virgin on Dec 25th. He was a travelling teacher who turned water into wine and was called 'Holy Child'! *Was that belief important?*

2000 yrs ago, in Judea, there was a man who, it is claimed, had many of the godly characteristics of the examples above. *Was that belief important? Why?*

"I contend that we are both atheists. I just believe in one fewer god than you do. When you understand why you dismiss all the other possible gods, you will understand why I dismiss yours."
Stephen Roberts

Our beliefs (the ideas in our heads) have no significance in the 'Greater Scheme of Things'.

However, they seem very important for 'Mankind's Machinations', in other words, for our social activities and for each of us personally. *So, how important are we?*

How important are we?
Each of us is but one individual in a current population of over 7 billion. That's a big number - it would take about 300 years of non-stop counting to get to 7 billion.

Since Homo sapiens evolved, about 100 billion of us have set foot on the Earth. Each one of us is numerically insignificant, like an ant.

When you have accepted the fact that, individually, we are as unimportant as ants, it is interesting to consider what value each 'ant' might have. Each of us 'ants' may live for about 80 years, whereas our species has existed for about 200,000 years, while planet Earth and the Solar System have been around for 4.6 billion years, and the Universe is about 13.8 billion years old. So in terms of astronomical time, geological time, or even in comparison to the period of existence of our species, we each survive for a trivial duration. *Isn't it vainglorious to imagine that we are important in our brief lives? Arrogant even?*

So how important is belief?

Do you think we can assign importance to ideas in our heads during our brief, numerically insignificant lives?

I think not! Our beliefs are monumentally unimportant, certainly in terms of the 'greater scheme of things'. Let's summarise:

- We are insignificant individuals in a vast population of humans alive and dead.
- We survive for a short period of time relative to many measures of duration.
- We can change our beliefs on a whimsy, for personal reasons.

If you want to assign importance to the beliefs you hold in your life, you are asking the word 'belief' to have a double meaning – of special importance within your head and, as you gain distance and perspective, to have no importance at the general level. *Can it mean both at once?* Scientists don't like words that have two meanings...

Just Remember:

It doesn't matter how strong your belief is

It doesn't matter how many share your belief

It doesn't matter how long your belief has lasted

No amount of belief can turn an idea into a fact

What turns ideas into facts is.....

EVIDENCE!

What about faith?

Unfortunately, like 'belief', 'faith' is a word with two meanings and that is a source of confusion, which is sometimes deliberate. Believers like to use it to mean 'justified confidence' but to a scientist that is an alien concept. No scientist will ever say, 'I have faith in evolution' or 'I have faith in gravity'!

To a scientist, faith is an *unquestioned, unevidenced* belief; it's like a belief on steroids! It's the padlock on the strongbox of belief. But we have just seen how belief is valueless when applied to the 'big questions' of the origins of the universe and mankind, so faith must also be valueless in this context. Yes, I know a small percentage of intellectual theists will claim to question their faith - so they should!

Unquestioning has nothing to recommend it. Failing to question their orders is what enabled the Treblinka camp guards to exterminate 800,000 Jews without suffering from guilt. Failing to question their indoctrination and failing to question the promise of 72 virgins in afterlife is what motivated the 9/11 suicide pilots.

Unquestioning is only going to give you no answers. Would you take untested medicines? Beware of words that begin with 'un'; they are not going to deliver – I have 364 'unbirthdays' a year! It's particularly difficult to understand the thinking behind the idea that not questioning a belief makes it *stronger*! Like homeopathy, which attempts to persuade us that a medication can become more powerful the more you dilute it (!), this style of thinking turns commonsense on its head. Please, don't stop questioning!

Belief can be applied to ideas that have different levels of significance. *Principles* are one sort of premise that becomes the subject of belief; people believe in political principles such as human rights. That's fine; we should hold such principles dearly. Going down, the next lower level is *propositions*. A proposition should not be believed, it should be investigated. Then comes *choices*; they do not deserve to be afforded the significance that 'belief' attributes and finally comes *faith*, the most undeserving premise of all.

It takes a real effort, first to realise the triviality of belief and then to come to terms with that realisation. In the meantime, we bestow our belief, this inflated commodity bursting with its own self-importance, far too freely. We splatter it about like confetti. We offer our belief to propositions we barely know, let alone fully understand. We believe we have the winning lottery ticket; that our horse will win the race; that breaking a mirror will bring seven years of bad luck.

Very few of us insist on the fulfilment of any conditions such as the support of convincing evidence before wilfully offering our belief to a proposition. Interestingly, if we did set the passing of the 'evidence test' as a criterion, we might arrive at an outcome that does not require belief – a fact!

Summary

We are individually insignificant; each of us is just a single person in a total human population (alive and dead) of about 100 billion, therefore our personal beliefs are unimportant. We have a fleeting existence of about 80 years out of the 200 thousand years of mankind's tenure on this planet, in all that time many more religions have died out than currently survive.

Deduction:

Religions are manmade and subject to changes in fashion and social conditions.

Conclusions:

1. Belief is monumentally unimportant. At best it is no more than a personal choice, at worst it has been imposed by parents, social pressure or the state.
2. Faith is just a set of beliefs held with more determination but no better justification.

COMPARISON OF SCIENTIFIC FACTS AND RELIGIOUS BELIEFS

FACTS	BELIEFS
Supported by evidence.	No supporting evidence.
Evidence in the form of *repeatable observations*.	No repeatable observations.
Are *discovered* through *investigations* sometimes involving *experiments*.	Not investigation based – just repetition or reinterpretation of ancient doctrines (ideas).
No believers required.	Believers essential.
Independent existence – can be rediscovered.	Only exist in men's heads, therefore subjective.
Were present before mankind existed.	Began when individuals first imagined them.
Will still be present after mankind becomes extinct.	Die when individuals change their minds or die themselves.
Describe and explain observed data/information.	Attempt to describe and explain unsubstantiated stories.
Enable predictions that, after verification, confirm fact as true.	Predictions are fantastic/eccentric or mundane/boring.
Rational and trustworthy.	Irrational and untrustworthy.
Often enable applications leading to products that empower mankind beyond bodily capabilities	No products. Social application of beliefs often leads to division and conflict.

4. EVIDENCE

What is it exactly?
'Data on which to base proof or to establish truth or falsehood.'
www.thefreedictionary.com

Unlike belief, evidence is not merely a proposition, not just an idea inside men's heads. It really exists independently, to be discovered and rediscovered, in the external environment. That's why it does not require believing.

How do we get evidence?
From OBSERVATIONS.

Historically, men only had their sense organs to make observations with – eyes, ears, nose, tongue and skin. If they had no evidence, they resorted to their imaginations and produced speculative responses to questions which cannot properly be described as answers. If you've ever spent time with young questioning children, you'll know the temptation to make up 'answers' just for some peace and quiet!

Since the time of the late bronze and early iron-age, when many 'modern' religions were originated, we have invented many tools to improve on our senses – telescopes, microscopes, X-ray cameras, Geiger counters, etc. Such instruments have enabled us to discover many things that the authors of 'holy scriptures' did not know existed such as galaxies, bacteria, dinosaurs, nuclear radiation; Biblical times were a profoundly ignorant period in man's history.

If I reported to you that I had observed fairies at the bottom of my garden, would you believe me? I doubt it. Wouldn't you insist, like Scientists do, that observations must be repeatable? Wouldn't you say, "Show me!"?

Repeatable Observations

Scientists are very sceptical – if something has only happened once or has only been observed by one person then, according to them, it simply hasn't happened. Well, it may have happened actually but without repeatable observations there is no *evidence* that it happened. That's healthy, sceptical thinking.

If other people could discover my fairies independently, maybe using different detectors, would you believe they existed? Surely, if they really existed, we should be able to observe my fairies repeatedly – rediscovery. It might mean data could be collected.

If different people, at different times, or in different places, or using different instruments, can independently repeat observations and get similar results, that is considered to be convincing evidence. If they get different results, that's also considered to be convincing evidence – that the hypothesis is incorrect!

Repeatable Observations are the strongest form of evidence. It's **The Gold Standard.**

Physical Evidence is also strong: bones and fossils, fingerprints, spent cartridges, traces of DNA. After all, such physical evidence can be repeatedly observed, but it has to be treated with respect. Detectives have to provide evidence which can be shown to judges or jurors – re-observed, so it has to be collected very carefully, bagged up (wearing gloves) and signed for by everyone who handles it, to establish a 'Chain of Responsibility' and eliminate the possibility of tampering.

Personal Experience
Sadly, an individual's experience cannot be shared and we know it is very easy to deceive the brain. Hallucinations can be stimulated by dreams, drugs, exercise, fever, blindness, illnesses, migraines, magnetic pulses, flashes, hypnotists, optical illusions, sensory deprivation and blows on the head. *How would*

you tell an imagined experience from a real one? What makes experiences valueless as evidence is there is no way of telling one from the other.

Experience is a very tender subject – people get offended if they feel their experiences are being denigrated. *Is seeing for oneself the only acceptable form of evidence though? Can we rely on our brains? And should we take the word of someone who seems to be a reliable witness?*

> *Nullius in Verba*
> The motto of the Royal Society
> (Take no-one's word for it, which applies to both the spoken and the written word)

Well, no. Sadly, our brains are standalone computers – there is no file sharing capability. This means that your experience may be valid for you and mine for me, but they are not interchangeable as evidence. Personal experience is just that, *personal* – it's subjective. We can learn skills from each other by mimicry – indeed, it's the best way. We can learn from each other's experience if we give our co-operation to a teacher, but when claims are being made against the propositions of rivals we need more stringent tests. Repeatable observations are convincing, experiences are not. So experiences are useless as sources of information.

The trouble is, since there is no file sharing, we can only communicate by language which is an imperfect tool. Sometimes there are no words to express an experience; sometimes, if time has passed between the experience and the telling of it, details are forgotten; sometimes the teller exaggerates his account to make it more entertaining; sometimes people lie or are simply mistaken. So accounts of experiences are untrustworthy.

In answer to those who ask, *"When Scientists read the dials on their instruments, is that not an experience?"* Well, yes it is; it is a different sort of experience. The number nine on the dial may have a special significance for you; it may be your birthday, while having no significance for me. We all have different experiences but we all have the *same* understanding of data. We will both record the number nine, furthermore the digital output from the instrument can be recorded or shared on the internet – is it a *personal* experience anymore? And, don't forget, any wild claims will be disputed in the repeatability and Peer Review process of Scientific Method.

Testimony

Little credibility is given to single witness accounts in court. *Why would you accept one man's word?* Men can exaggerate, forget, lie, or simply be mistaken.

That's why, in a court of law, one man's word is not usually taken against another's; it never should be in my opinion – who are we to judge one man's veracity against another man's? Maybe if scientific standards of evidence were required in court there would be fewer unsafe convictions...

We can't trust testimonies – men telling of their experiences are performing before an audience and, naturally, they like to make the story more gripping by embellishing it; every time it is retold it gets 'better', i.e. *less accurate!* It takes few repeats for this to happen.

Scientists are not immune to this; some have been known to fiddle their results in the pursuit of glory; Cyril Burt was a researcher into intelligence whose reputation was ruined when it was discovered, after his death, that he had falsified his results.

Personal experience and testimony are unacceptable as convincing evidence. Identification parades are also notoriously unreliable – in a test, only 7 out of 54 witnesses identified the culprit! Check out this video: http://www.youtube.com/watch?v=gBbs2tTDs7U

Separate witnesses are notoriously unreliable and can be interfered with – we have to prevent them from meeting and agreeing their story in advance, or from

being influenced by one side or the other. Even expert witnesses are now treated with suspicion following Sir Roy Meadow's fall from grace. See link:
http://en.wikipedia.org/wiki/Roy_Meadow

Multiple Witnesses

As outlined above, if different people in different places or times observe the same phenomenon that counts as a repeated observation. An example would be the around 300 victims of paedophile Jimmy Savile who all reported the same modus operandi over a period of forty years but, if a group of people all claim to have had the same experience *together*, we must be on the lookout for cheating. *Were they all influenced by drugs, or by a charismatic leader, or by an illusionist, or are they in someone's pay?*

Illusionists and Magicians sometimes use accomplices to enhance their tricks. So it's best to be sceptical, especially if the claims contravene the Laws of Physics. See video:
http://www.youtube.com/watch?v=422M4WixG9I

'Faith healers' have also been caught using an accomplice too. See video:
http://www.youtube.com/watch?v=q7BQKu0YP8Y

Recorded 'Evidence'

Writing was the first means of recording (apart from cave paintings), so books contain some of our earliest reports. Centuries later, picture and sound recording methods were invented. Fiction is a record of the author's imagination; unfortunately, sometimes it's mixed up with non-fiction. This is why the expression 'in black and white' is no guarantee of veracity.

Without verification, audio and pictorial records are not accepted in courts because they can easily be falsified with Photoshop, iMovie and similar software. Books should also be regarded with suspicion – I am modifying this text right now! They are records, not evidence, unless verified.

Verification

It's easy to verify a telephone directory – just make a few calls. Science text books can also be verified – simply repeat the experiments that led to the information they contain. Religious books cannot be verified – you are expected to believe them by an act of 'faith'.

'Scriptures'

'Scriptures' just means 'writings'. Using a special word for writing about a particular subject is an obvious attempt to make it seem more important. The same applies to the custom of capitalising the words 'god' and 'lord'; it is an attempt to make the concepts seem important, grandiose and *real*. The spurious use of capitals should be a clue to invalidity. Speech and writing were invented by humans, not a 'god' and books are just manmade records, not evidence of anything unless verified.

Religious books are not even testable let alone verifiable and they were written decades after the events they report – *have you heard of 'Chinese whispers'?* Here is a famous example:

Captain in trenches to messenger, *"Say to the General, send reinforcements we're going to advance!"*
Messenger to General, *"Send three and four pence*, we're going to a dance!"*

* Three shillings and four pence in old UK £sd.

You can't expect the oral tradition to be a source of accurate information even after it has been written down. Especially if it's not written at the time, Chinese whispers begin in minutes - just watch breaking news.

"Ancient religious texts are not sources of information, the concept is ridiculous."
Professor A C Grayling

Furthermore, the 'explanations' for the 'big questions of life' found in different parts of the 'scriptures' disagree with each other and are contradicted by evidence. Not only that but, as already noted, many of the accounts of purported events in the scriptures even contravene the Laws of Physics; such incredible stories may have been persuasive to goat-herders in the past but they do not serve their purpose well in the educated societies of the twenty-first century!

The Bible was edited in the 4th century AD under the command of Emperor Constantine and it has been translated, transcribed and re-edited many times since. The tacit remit of the editors of the famous King James' version was to make it a more powerful tool to fulfil their paymaster's (the King's) wishes to satisfy his subject's need for a 'spiritual life' and make them easier to govern. If people believe in a heavenly afterlife, they will tolerate more abuse during their real existence! The editors needed to make the King's bible into an effective marketing tool or they might have incurred his displeasure! They knew that Kings executed people!

So the Bible sows seeds of fear and guilt whilst promising 'salvation' to its own non-evidential threats! It promotes a bronze-age morality which condones acts that are criminal today but which provided gory stories for attracting people to church – the entertainment centres of the past. Whilst they are worshipping, the King's subjects can't be rioting! The King James Bible proved to be very persuasive right up to the nineteenth century when it played a significant role in the British colonisation of West Africa.

The Koran dates back to the 6th century and also recommends social mores which are unacceptable today. Society is far less brutal now than it was in the time when those books were written.

Ok, religion has been the inspiration for commissioning wonderful works of art and much great music (and so has love, madness, nature, power, war and fantasy) but I contend that religious thinking has provided *no knowledge at all*, no products, and no services which are not also capable of being provided secularly. *Do you agree with that statement or can you think of any products, services or scraps of evidence-based knowledge that have been provided exclusively by a religion?*

On the other side of the scales, no one could deny that evidence derived by following Scientific Method really works! Just look at all the benefits that knowledge obtained by Scientific Method has given us. We have exceeded our bodily capabilities in many ways – we can fly! We have put a flag on the moon! We can chat with people around the world from the comfort of our own homes! We can replace a diseased heart!

However, evidence comes with two caveats: scientific investigations usually result in more questions than answers and the outcomes only provide probability, not proof. Proof is only for mathematicians and crime fiction writers.

Never forget that scientific facts are based on a consensus of expert opinion founded on convincing evidence, nothing more, certainly not on proof. That's why all scientific knowledge is constantly up for review; that's how Einstein was able to make improvements to Newton's model of gravity.

Sadly, our brains, 'wired' to search for solutions, find the lack of proof unsettling. That's why faiths are so easy to sell with their black and white 'certainties', even though they are unsupported by evidence and therefore open to being regarded as bogus. No evidence of any worthwhile standard has ever been produced to support the proposition that there is any god; not a Zeus, an Anubis, a Cloacina, an Ixcacao nor a Jesus.

However, the absence of evidence is not evidence of absence; no-one can *prove* a negative proposition. If you ask me to *prove* there is no elephant in this room, the best I can do is say there is no evidence of an elephant. That's why the onus is on the proposer to supply evidence or face scepticism. The leaders of religions find themselves in this difficult position; they lack evidence, that's why they need faith and dogma.

There has been no evidence produced to support the claim that there is any god throughout all of history, that's why so many beliefs in old gods have died out. If there was some evidence, wouldn't the priests have grasped it with open hands? If it had been discovered wouldn't they have trumpeted it? Wouldn't they have looked after it and shown it to everyone? Wouldn't it supersede their shaky reliance on 'faith'?

Everyone recognises the value of evidence – we use it to determine guilt, to evaluate treatments and medications, to evaluate markets for potential products, etc. Emperor Constantine even sent one of his women to the 'holy land' to search for evidence to support Christianity when he decided to adopt it as the Roman Empire's state religion. Religions would love to have the evidence that science has – some of them have even paid homage by incorporating 'science' into their name, e.g. Christian Scientists and Scientology.

Evidence is conclusive. When you have it, your work is almost done; you just need to point to it. Faith on the other hand, being an unevidenced belief, requires constant work to buttress it as it, rightly, comes under attack from doubters. Priests have to perpetually publicly assert their doctrine in a dogmatic way – the job is never done.

Many religious leaders have been reported revealing their true thoughts:

- Former Bishop of Durham, David Jenkins, said he did not believe in the physical resurrection of Christ or the virgin birth.
- Archbishop of Canterbury, Rowan Williams, said, *"The three wise men are just a legend".* Our children are being taught otherwise.
- RC Archbishop of Sydney, Cardinal Pell, said, *"The biblical story of Adam and Eve is a myth constructed for religious purposes."*
- Retired Bishop of Newark, John Shelby Spong, said, *"Hell is an invention of the church. The church is in the fear and control business."*
- Pope Benedict XVII said, *"Limbo was just a theological concept."*
- Pope Leo Xth is reported as saying, *"The fable of Christ has been quite profitable to us."*

And so on...

Summary

Convincing evidence only comes in one form: repeatable observations. Anecdotes, experiences, and testimonials do not count as convincing evidence. Books are records, not evidence, unless verified. Ideas lacking the support of evidence remain just propositions and do not achieve the status of facts unless convincing evidence is provided.

There is no doubt that evidence is good stuff; if you were wrongly accused of murder, you'd be demanding it, wouldn't you?

"Religion is something left over from the infancy of our intelligence, it will fade away as we adopt Reason and Science as our guidelines."
Bertrand Russell

Celebrity Quote:

"Don't you believe in flying saucers, they ask me? Don't you believe in telepathy? In ancient astronauts? In the Bermuda Triangle? In life after death?

I reply, No, no, no, no, and again no. One person recently, goaded into desperation by my litany of unrelieved negation, burst out, Don't you believe in anything? Yes, I said. I believe in evidence. I believe in observation, measurement and reasoning, confirmed by independent observers. I'll believe anything, no matter how wild and ridiculous, if there is evidence for it. The wilder and more ridiculous something is, however, the firmer and more solid the evidence will have to be."

Isaac Asimov 1920 -1992

5. WHAT IS SCIENCE?

Many people don't understand what Science is and how it works, so there follows a short explanation:

What is Science?
Unlike other subjects, Science is not merely a body of knowledge, it's a *process*. Instead of just believing what they were told when they were children because it was written in some ancient book, *Scientists seek evidence* to support proposed answers to questions.

> *"Science is a way of thinking much more than it is a body of knowledge"*
> **Carl Sagan**

I found this excellent definition of Science on comedian Robin Ince's blog: *'A self-correcting, evidence based system of exploring the universe which attempts to unearth the least wrong laws and theories that can explain what exists or might exist whilst accepting that room must always be left for doubt and further enquiry.'*

Before the introduction of Science, when faced with a question, somebody just guessed at the answer and told their children, probably to shut them up! That answer then got passed down the generations. This is how religious doctrine originates.

Scientific method often *starts* in the same way, with a guess (hypothesis) but then *an investigation is carried out to test the guess*; observations are made, evidence is collected. Religions omit the investigation stage.

The Scientific Process goes like this:
1. Decide on a question.
2. Suggest possible solutions (Hypotheses - educated guesses).
3. Construct an Investigation to test a Hypothesis.
4. Make observations (preferably using instruments to collect data).
5. Repeat the Investigation to eliminate fluke results.
6. Draw conclusions, suggest predictions and submit for publication to a peer reviewed journal.
7. Other Scientists repeat investigations and confirm (or deny) results.
8. Scientific community comes to agreement about the discovery.
9. If contrary evidence is ever discovered, the process goes back to the hypothesising stage.

When the majority of scientists are convinced, the proposition is accepted as a fact and further research can be pursued.

Common Misconceptions about Science

- *"Scientists are know-alls who think they can explain everything"*

WRONG! If scientists had the answers to all the questions they would stop investigating! There would be nothing left to do. In fact, the more we discover, the more questions occur to us - just ask a researcher!

- *"Science is just a belief like religions"*

WRONG! Scientific facts do not require belief. They exist outside of men's heads and can be discovered and rediscovered by anyone, anywhere and at any time. They are 'owned' by everyone who has been informed and are not the property of individuals, unlike a 'personal god'.

- *"Scientists can prove things."*

WRONG! Scientists only provide evidence. Good scientists don't like to use the word 'proof'. Ok, some scientific facts have a very high probability of being correct - e.g. *'The heart pumps blood around the circulatory system',* but we don't like to close the door on the possibility that new evidence may turn up and we might have to revise our view. This happened with Newton's Theory of Gravity (which still works pretty well within the Solar System) when

Einstein came up with his Theory of Relativity which is slightly more accurate in deep space. Scientists like to keep open minds. They would even consider the proposition that there may be a god if you provided them with some evidence!

- *"Evolution is only a Theory"*

WRONG! The scientific usage of the word 'theory' is quite different from the way it is used in everyday language. It doesn't mean a guess! The scientific word for (educated) guess is hypothesis. A Scientific Theory is supported by plenty of convincing evidence and a consensus of agreement by experts worldwide. It also enables predictions that can be tested to confirm or deny its claims.

IN FACT, THE USE OF SCIENTIFIC METHOD HAS PROVIDED US WITH EVERYTHING WE KNOW.

Even before scientific method was formalised, people discovered information by unwittingly using it!

Yes, some scientific discoveries have been put to bad use. Science and technology empower mankind, that's what they do. If men choose to use this power to do bad things that's not the scientists' fault; blame the policy makers – politicians and terrorists. Remember, even a stick can be used either to sow seeds or bash someone on the head – you can't blame the stick!

Alfred Nobel, inventor of dynamite, felt so guilty about the way he was described as 'The Agent of Death' in his mistakenly premature obituary (it was his brother who had actually died!) that he left funds in his will for those who confer the 'greatest benefit to mankind', hence the annual Nobel Prizes.

Similar thinking has resulted in some fields of research, which could lead in dangerous directions for society, not being pursued. This is why we have ethical committees overseeing research funding applications.

Please note that, although Science is based on evidence, the conclusions made are not regarded to be proven, they are just considered to be *probable* and are open to revision if new evidence comes in. Consequently, there is no absolute 'truth' – see next Chapter.

Summary

The best sort of evidence comes from repeatable observations, preferably using instruments to yield quantitative data. The proposition that there is a god cannot meet that standard.

More Celebrity Quotes:

"If people are good only because they fear punishment and hope for reward, then we are a sorry lot indeed"
Albert Einstein

§

"Atheists are routinely asked how people will know not to rape and murder without religion telling them not to do it, especially a religion that backs up the orders with threats of hell. Believers, listen to me carefully when I say this: When you use this argument, you terrify Atheists. We hear you saying that the only thing standing between you and Ted Bundy (a serial killer and rapist) is a flimsy belief in a supernatural being made up by pre-literate people trying to figure out where the rain came from. This is not very reassuring if you're trying to argue from a position of moral authority."
Amanda Marcotte

* Amanda got one thing wrong – the bible does not disapprove of rape specifically! (See later)

§

"People often ask me, 'If there is no god, what is there to stop us from raping and killing each other as much as we want?' I answer that I have raped and killed as much as I want – which is zero."
Penn Jillette

6. THE QUEST FOR 'TRUTH'

What is 'truth'?
'Something that accords with fact.'
Merriam-Webster's Online Dictionary

Humans love the concept of truth. The way our brains have evolved to search for answers, to be hopeful about finding them and to be persistent in the hunt, leads us to desire an absolute result; an absolute truth.

If only the reality was that simple! Take a look at the following examples:

1. One night I showed my daughter the moon. She said, "It's moving." I said, "No, it's the clouds that are moving, see – the moon is still the same distance from that roof." Was that true? Two hours later the moon had clearly moved away from the roof. Is that true?

We now know that the moon orbits the earth and the earth rotates on its axis; the earth rotates once a day, the moon orbits once in 28 days. Which effect is *truly* responsible for those observations?

2. What will happen if a billiard table is not flat? What will happen if it's not level?

To stop the balls all rolling to one spot, we make billiard tables as 'true', i.e. flat and level, as possible. Now let's alter the scale: let's make the table 10,000 miles long. If it's truly flat and level, the balls will all roll to the middle because, due to the curvature of the earth's surface, gravity will pull them 'down' there to get nearest to the ground! On that scale the table needs to be horizontal (parallel with the horizon) that is, not flat and level, but domed!

3. If a wall is not built vertically it will fall over. *True or false?* The walls of a building are usually built parallel (except for The Shard): *True or False?* So two walls can be simultaneously vertical and parallel: *True or False?*

Well, again, it depends on the scale – because, since the earth is a globe, vertical actually means radiating from the centre and, if a wall is on a radius it cannot be parallel to another radial wall! If it *is* parallel to another wall, one or both of them will not be radial and, if built tall enough for the centre of gravity to be outside the footprint, will fall over!

4. A moving train blows its whistle. *What will a passenger on board hear? What will a person standing by the track hear as it goes past? Which is true?*

This is the effect explained by Herr Doppler. A person standing still by the track experiences the sound waves compressed to a higher frequency due to the approaching speed of the source then, as the train passes and recedes into the distance, the waves are stretched apart to a lower frequency. A person travelling on the train will hear a constant pitch. Both are true to the observers in their own locations: one moving, the other static.

In those examples, the 'truth', as perceived by an observer, depends on context, particularly scale, location and movement.
Conclusion: External truth is relative! It's subjective – your 'truth' may be different to mine.

The 'truth' is we live in an illusion that has been created for us by our own sense organs and brain. For example, 'now' doesn't exist! *"How can that be?"* I hear you ask. OK, let's dissect 'now': it's easy to say, but *when* is it exactly? Is it when you say the *'n'* or the *'ow'*? If we recorded you saying *'now'* and examined the waveform, we could ask, *'Is it at the beginning of the 'n' or some fraction of a second later?'*

The hand of time is never stopped so, if we sample smaller and smaller slices of time, although we can say that this slice was before the moment of 'now' and the next one was after, there is no stationary slice in between! The 'cusp' of the present does not exist!

Then, the reality is, it takes about 300 milliseconds for our brains to process the signals coming in from our sense organs so we live in the past! By the time we are experiencing 'now', it's gone!

Another problem is the incoming signals do not all arrive simultaneously! Messages from the nose and ears reach the brain first because they have a very short journey, whereas the sensory nerves from your tip of your foot, which tells you when you are touching the floor, are about 2 metres long. The brain has to convene a meeting of neurons and negotiate a compromise approximation of 'now'!

It gets even more complicated when you realise that the different parts of your body do not experience 'now' in the same timeframe! You are on a planet that rotates at 1000 mph (at the equator), so your 'top' i.e. the bit furthest from the ground, is travelling faster and therefore ageing more slowly than the part of you touching the surface of the Earth. The effect is tiny of course, but slightly greater when you are standing up than when lying down! So ageing is affected by height and altitude and attitude! If we had one clock on our head and another on one of our feet, the head clock would run minutely slower! Doing a handstand would reverse the effect!

Experiments with two identical, very accurate, clocks, one kept on the ground while the other takes a flight in a fast aircraft, have verified this effect in practice. Less time passes for the travelling clock. It's not the same as one clock simply being in a different time zone; in this case the actual units of time are longer for the slower clock. Time is relative – we can only say an hour is longer by comparing it with another hour that is shorter! It's as if one clock is in a different universe which has a slower tick! To get to this 'other universe' you simply have to move faster. It doesn't matter where you go, it could be in a circle! Of course, you are already travelling in a circle as the Earth rotates and your head is going faster than your feet...

Have you ever shaken hands or been kissed? Did you feel the solidity of the other person? No you didn't! 'Solid' is not real at the quantum level! Every substance is made of atoms which consist of a nucleus surrounded by orbiting electrons. In between the nucleus and the electrons there is nothing. Atoms are 99% nothing! What you experienced was the repulsive forces between *your* outermost electrons and *their* outermost electrons. You are repulsive! Ever sat on a chair? No you haven't! You've hovered over it!

So obviously, in the greater scheme of things, truth is relative to scale, location and motion. *However, when we ask our children to tell the truth we know what we mean, don't we? Is it the case that in applications to do with the mere social doings of mankind (e.g. 'Who is guilty?'), 'perceived' truth seems to have an absolute meaning, but for questions of greater significance in the wider universe it can only muster a relative meaning? Is 'truth' another word, like 'believe' that has two meanings depending on its context?*

Is it a word that is subjectively absolute but objectively relative? How can something subjective be absolute? Surely it depends on the circumstances of the subject: the observer? Man's truth, the social 'truth' that we run our communities on, is subjective. It depends on the point of view of the observer. Your freedom fighter might be my terrorist.

Conclusion: *All* truth is personal and relative.

Summary

External objective truth is a slippery concept; it is relative. Even the Laws of Physics that we regard as 'Universal Truths' are only true because they haven't been falsified yet. *Will the speed of light prove not to be absolute one day?* We don't know how it behaves inside a black hole yet...

"Few who first meet religion as an adult can take it seriously"
Prof A C Grayling

"No testimony is sufficient to establish a miracle, unless the testimony be of such a kind that its falsehood would be <u>more</u> miraculous."
David Hume, Scottish Philosopher.

"Religion is something left over from the infancy of our intelligence, it will fade away as we adopt Reason and Science as our guidelines."

***

"Where there is evidence, no one speaks of 'faith'. We do not speak of faith that two and two are four or that the earth is round. We only speak of faith when we wish to substitute emotion for evidence."
Bertrand Russell

"The presence of those seeking the truth is infinitely to be preferred to the presence of those who think they've found it!"
Terry Pratchett

"More people have been killed in the name of Jesus Christ than in any other name in the history of the world."
Gore Vidal

7. ORIGIN OF THE UNIVERSE

One of the big stumbling blocks in any debate with many believers is the origin of the universe. Different religions have their various stories of creation. Here are just a few:

Australian Aboriginals have 'The Maker of Many Things' who brought creatures and human ancestors from under the ground and over the seas during 'Dreamtime'. They say the sun is an Emu's egg that the Eagle threw up into the sky where it burst into flame! These stories are secret and sacred and are passed on orally.

Taoism has a story of chaos being changed by the creative power of Yin and Yang. Out of the mist came a great colourful light, the mist shook and separated, everything light went up to form heaven and everything heavy fell to form the earth. The forces of yin and yang created a giant, 'P'an Ku', who dug the river valleys and piled up the mountains. The hard work killed him and his hair became the plants, his blood became rivers while his parasites became humans!

Jews, and Christians claim that, in the beginning, god created the universe in one week. He said, 'Let there be light' on the first day, and made the heavens on the second day. On the third day he raised dry land from the water below and brought forth plants. The fourth day was when he named the bright light 'day' and the dim light 'night'. Day five saw him fill the sea with creatures and the air with birds. The sixth day was very busy – he created all kinds of land animals including mankind, so on the seventh day he rested; an all powerful god needs rest apparently – I hope you don't ever need him while he is sleeping!

The Hindu creation story assumes there have been several worlds and universes. Lord Brahma the Creator made the universes, Lord Vishnu the Preserver maintains them and Lord Shiva is the destroyer and re-creator. These three are all part of the Supreme One (is this where the Christian idea of the 'Holy Trinity' came from?). Chaos is followed by a creation and then destruction brings back chaos – this pattern cycles repeatedly (allegedly).

Muslims have a variation of the Abrahamic story found in the Old Testament. They say god made the world, the heavens and all the creatures that walk, swim, crawl or fly on the earth. He made it rain, broke up the soil and brought forth the corn, olive trees, palm trees and grass. He ordered angels to land on Earth and bring back seven handfuls of soil which he moulded into a man called Adam and breathed life into him. He made Eve from Adam's rib. One angel went rogue, disobeyed god, and tempted Eve to eat the forbidden fruit (talking snakes are Christian!). God cast them out of Paradise to live on Earth until they served him well.

The Sanema people of the Amazon believe their ancestors were created long ago by Omao. He wanted to make humans from hardwood trees but his brother Soawe was lazy and provided more easily obtainable softwood. Omao was cross saying he wanted to make humans from hardwood so they would live forever, "I was going to use softwood for the anaconda so they would die young." That is why people do not live forever, apparently. In anger, Omao left the world and went to the bottom of the sky. *Where's that?*

There are many other beliefs about the origin of the universe and, strangely, these wildly different accounts are all correct according to their supporters! That's despite such incongruities as for example, in the biblical account, god creating the light on day one but not creating the sun, the source of light, until day four! *Are they nothing more than ignorant guesses?*

Scientists say there is good evidence to indicate that the universe began in a 'Big Bang' about 13.8 billion years ago. It's true that we don't understand all the loose ends yet, but that's no reason to invent a god.

Please notice that none of these creation stories comes with evidence. They don't mention it. They are just presented as a story. Now, you might think that would be a handicap to their credibility. Unfortunately not: these stories are fed to children at a young age and they are often unchallenged later in life. Information fed to children early gets absorbed into memory far easier and at a deeper level; as such it is more difficult to dispute at a personal level later in life (see Post Script). There are reasons the Jesuits have the saying, *'Give me a boy of seven and I'll show you the man'!* They don't mention females though!

Now here's a confession! I'm not easily annoyed but there's one thing that does aggravate me: it's Double Standards! Especially when exhibited by believers who seem prepared to walk past the myriad benefits of Science, which have enabled mankind to vastly exceed his bodily capabilities, to point at the frontiers of knowledge and crow, *"Na na ne na na! Science can't explain the Big Bang!"*

How can believers expect the highest level of perfect understanding and supporting evidence from Science while overlooking the total lack of those qualities from their own propositions?* I say to them, *"I'll show you the evidence we have so far that supports the Big Bang Theory and then you must show me the evidence for Creation."*

The existence of a 'Creator' is just a proposition. No matter how often and how strongly it is asserted, it will remain merely a proposition until it is supported by evidence.

Please notice also that the story of creation proposes one answer to several questions. The question of the origin of the universe (or visible 'heavens' as it was at the time) is bundled together with the question of the origin of life and the question of how life diversified into so many different forms. The single proposed answer is goddunnit. Science addresses these questions separately and does not attempt a simplistic answer.

Evidence for the Big Bang

I'm going to deal with this historically because the sequence of discoveries lends a context to what we know today.

In the beginning (☺), men looked up and saw what appeared to be a dome of sky above them across which the sun traversed daily and on which the moon went through phases mostly at night. Naturally, they concluded that the sun and moon went around the Earth – after all, that is what appears to be happening. When the sun set they imagined it went underneath the Earth, which as far as they could see, was flat, and climbed back into the sky on the other side next morning.

Given that the naked eye was their only means of making observations, a dome of sky was an entirely reasonable assumption. This was the extent of understanding in the days of the 'prophets' and remained the case right up until Galileo made the first telescope to be usefully pointed at the sky thousands of years later.

What Galileo saw, in 1610, was that Venus had phases like the moon so he realised that, like the moon, it reflected light from the sun. That gave him reason to conclude that the planets orbited the sun which confirmed the view first expressed by Copernicus in 1543. By then the 'sky dome' notion had become part of the doctrine of the church so, when Galileo declared that the earth was not the centre of the universe (they knew nothing of the existence of other galaxies then), he was locked up for heresy! Church leaders brook no disagreement!

Searching the sky with his telescope enabled Galileo to observe that the Milky Way, which appears as a smear to the naked eye, was actually composed of a vast number of stars. That's when he realised that the Solar System was merely a tiny corner of a vast universe. Isaac Newton also had this idea and published his opinion that the Universe is infinite and static; he was a rather unorthodox Christian and this suited his belief system. That outlook was widely accepted until the beginning of the twentieth century. Newton's Laws of Motion were developed into a Theory of Gravity which enabled the calculation of the planet's orbits and the prediction of the return dates of comets.

Then it was found that the planet Mercury did not behave according to how the calculations said it should. Enter Albert Einstein; in 1915 he came up with his new theory of General Relativity, which explained why Mercury orbited faster than Newton's equations predicted. However, the General Relativity equations suggested that the Universe should either contract or expand, which went against the thinking of the time.

In the intervening time, better telescopes had been developed and, in 1750, English astronomer Thomas Wright, noticed some unusual 'stars' that he called spiral 'nebulae' from the Latin for 'cloud'. Five years later, German Philosopher Immanuel Kant suggested that they might be 'island universes' like the Milky Way, but his idea was neglected until Vesto Slipher made a precision spectroscope that enabled the light from stars to be analysed for the first time.

By then, the spectra emitted and absorbed by different elements had been studied so it was possible to recognise the dark lines in the spectra of starlight, rather like a modern day bar code, and to identify the elements that far away stars are made of. When they obtained a detailed spectrum of the spiral nebula, Andromeda, they noticed that the 'barcodes' were moved towards the blue end of the spectrum. Calculations showed that this meant Andromeda was hurtling towards us at 300km per second!

Slipher soon gathered more data which showed that many other galaxies were red-shifted indicating they are moving away from us at up to 1000km/sec! At the time, distances in space could not be calculated – how could you tell whether a star was nearby and dim, or far away and bright?

Then, in 1912, Henrietta Swan Leavitt identified a type of star that enables us to determine its distance. The 'Cepheids' vary in brightness over a period of time (even our own sun varies by 0.1% over an 11 year Solar Cycle). She discovered that the periodicity of the

Cepheid's variation in brightness was related to their overall luminosity – the brighter they are, the more slowly their brightness varies. If you measure the period of variation (the pulse), you can calculate how bright they would be if they shone constantly and, if you measure how bright they actually look on average, the difference between the two enables you to work out how far away they are (light intensity obeys the inverse square rule).

These useful stars became known as 'standard candles'. They were used to work out that the 'spiral nebulae' were actually large galaxies in their own right and that they were outside the Milky Way, not just little stars inside it. Telescopes kept improving and work continued until Edwin Hubble was able to show that the further away a star is, the more its 'barcode' spectrum is red-shifted (The Hubble Constant). This means that distant galaxies are receding from us at high velocity.

In 1927, Georges Lemaitre suggested an explanation for this expansion: he said it's like an 'explosion'. Fred Hoyle named it the 'Big Bang' (that's a very bad name but journalists love it!). The information coming in enabled the calculation of the age of the Universe; it's like playing a video backwards and working out how long it took the galaxies, travelling at the speed they are doing, to get to where they are now.

The first attempts indicated that the Universe was 2 billion years old, which was a problem because other scientists had just uncovered evidence that the Earth was a similar age (we now know the Earth is actually 4.6 billion years old). For a while, a rival explanation to the Big Bang gained credence: Fred Hoyle's Steady State Theory which proposed that more, new, galaxies appeared in the space produced as the Universe expanded. Today, however, the measurements have been improved and now there is agreement that the Universe is about 13.76 billion years old.

Apart from red-shift, another strand of evidence supporting the Big Bang account of the origin of the Universe arrived in 1964 when the Cosmic Background Radiation was discovered to be 3 degrees Kelvin. This is the left over radiation from the original 'explosion'.

Recent observations involving a new type of 'standard candle', Type 1 supernovae, reveal that the expansion is speeding up, which is a loose end awaiting an explanation – *what's causing it?* We simply don't know.

Now, you may consider that you might pull on that loose thread and unravel the entire scientific explanation for the origin of the universe. Well, feel free! Scientists are doing that already! They are constructing possible alternative hypotheses and trying to unify our understanding of Cosmology with our understanding of Quantum Mechanics. Remember, that's how science works – by questioning everything; there are no Scientific Sacred Cows! I know this will be less than satisfactory for you certainty-seekers out there! You just need to get used to uncertainty!

In the meantime, we have an explanation for the origin supported by two major pieces of evidence (red shift and cosmic microwave background radiation) which enables the construction of a model that fits observations pretty closely. Any new, improved, model will probably be a development of this one and will have to agree with the existing evidence and any new observations that might come in.

Contrast this with the naïve 'god dunnit' Creationist's explanation. It's not supported by one shred of evidence unless you count stories in assorted implausible books written centuries ago when men were so ignorant they were unaware of the existence of bacteria and dinosaurs let alone other galaxies! (See earlier for why books are not evidence)

Ultimately, you have a choice; go with your preferred myth – Omao, P'an Ku, Lord Brahma, etc. or accept the Big Bang as a Theory supported by some convincing evidence which enables predictions that validate it. You can always revise your position, if and when more information comes in! That's perfectly acceptable – *indeed it's how science works*. I doubt that your priest would permit you a similar leeway!

Summary

The 'Big Bang', although it is misleadingly named, has considerable supporting evidence. Creationism has none. Science has a methodology for discovering information; part of the methodology is accepting criticism and being responsive to new evidence.

Religious Concepts for which there is no Evidence:

A Creator

A God

Souls

Heaven

Hell

Angels

Cherubs

Satan

Limbo (recently abolished by Pope Benedict)

Purgatory

Resurrection

Virgin Birth

Walking on Water

Turning water into wine

And many more...

8. EVOLUTION

The other bone of contention between many believers and Scientific Realists is evolution. This is despite 98% of scientists having signed up to it and also the Roman Catholic Church! Yes, Pope John Paul II stated there was no conflict between true (?!) science and religion in 1996 and then, in 2009, head of the Pontifical Council for Culture, Archbishop Gianfranco Ravasi, claimed Darwinism is compatible with the Christian view of Creation. He stole it from Darwin though, by saying that it could be traced to Saint Augustine and Saint Thomas Aquinas! This modified view seems to suggest that god kick-started life in an initial form and left it to get on with evolving. *How does that square with the claim that the bible is 'gospel truth', the 'word of god' and 'inerrant'? Is the Archbishop saying that Roman Catholics can't be fundamentalists?*

Unlike the 'Big Bang', the *scientific* explanation for the origin of the universe, the Judeo/Christian/Islamic creation story doesn't end at the creation of the universe (which was believed to be Earth centred at the time and much smaller due to the lack of knowledge of other galaxies) but it goes on to offer an 'explanation' for the existence of the whole variety of life on Earth. According to this hypothesis, god created all the different species of animals and plants in just four days of one week – Zap!

There are no bacteria or other micro-organisms in the biblical story of Creation; they were unknown to the authors because microscopes had not been invented when it was being written. Also, the lack of telescopes prevented the inclusion of other galaxies and extraterrestrial planets. Similarly, the Creation tale lacks any mention of dinosaurs or other fossils; the introduction of the science of palaeontology was thousands of years in the future. The scribes of the 'Holy Scriptures' were also unaware that 90% of the creatures that have ever existed are now extinct, so they didn't feel the need to explain why god had allowed this tragedy to happen to so many of his 'perfect' creations! But, they included nine mentions of unicorns and numerous references to dragons!

Of course, a corollary to the Creation proposition is that the species must be *fixed and unchanging* because god created them with beauty allegedly (e.g. a tapeworm?), which has been interpreted as perfection. That contention started to get questioned as selective breeding began to alter the characteristics of domesticated plants and animals; men were learning about heredity.

What is Evolution?

Believers tend to have a distorted view of evolution. In the same way that politicians like to misrepresent their opponent's policies, many believers like to scoff at evolutionists saying it's just random chance like monkeys typing Shakespeare! (Selection is not random chance, see later.) Another accusation they make is that evolution is 'just' a theory. That one merely reveals their ignorance of the meaning of the word 'Theory' in the scientific context (see Chapter 2).

Evolution simply means change. If you accept that you need a new flu vaccine each year because the flu virus has changed, you are accepting evolution. Also, evolution has nothing to say yet about the origin of life; that's another question. It merely explains the mechanism by which one species can evolve (change) into another, that's all. That mechanism is *natural* selection.

Selection itself is not a mystery; men have been selectively breeding animals and plants to make them into better 'products' for centuries. That's how we have got all the different breeds of dogs, fancy fish, fancy pigeons, roses and tulips, etc. That's how we got short stemmed wheat and maize that resist damage by wind, and dwarf peas that don't require supporting sticks and produce seven pods per stalk.

When I was young, the Christmas turkey carcass was tall and narrow; now they've been bred to be squatter. *Why?* Because people prefer the breast meat and ovens are square so, if the carcass is short and wide you can get a bigger breasted bird in. For the turkey farmers, who naturally want to sell more turkey, it was easier to change the shape of the turkey by selective breeding than to alter the proportions of all our ovens. Another example is wild hens, which occasionally produce an unfertilized egg while their domesticated descendants lay almost every day, thanks to selective breeding. That's how we have improved the yield of crops and farm animals. Here is an excellent video link: http://www.youtube.com/watch?v=GhHOjC4oxh8&feature=youtu.be

No one disputes that *'artificial'* (man instigated) selection works. Darwinian evolution merely says that selection, that is *the favouring of individuals with certain characteristics*, not only occurs when man interferes, but also happens naturally in response to environmental pressures and, since 'nature' has had much longer to do it, the changes have been rather larger. If a population of a hundred individuals contains ninety eight that are vulnerable to a new disease and two that are resistant, those two will be the ones that survive to pass on their resistant genes to their offspring; simples! *Where's the problem?*

The proposition that, over generations, animals and plants can change (or be changed) is so self-evident that you could be forgiven for thinking that a person would have to be peculiarly blinkered, short-sighted or closed minded to deny it!

Enter *heresy* – the (invented) 'crime' of disagreeing with religious doctrine, and *blasphemy* – the (invented) 'crime' of disrespecting 'Holy' personages; men have been imprisoned and executed for both. To me, the need to bolster a faith with rules like that is indicative of its illegitimacy and, if I believed in 'evil', I would apply that adjective to organised religions; since I don't believe in 'evil', I'm going to call them 'heinous'. Here is what a famous author who *is* happy to use the word 'evil' thinks:

"Religion is evil – morally and intellectually corrupt"
Louis de Bernieres
Author of Captain Corelli's Mandolin

Faced with the obvious evidence that a species can be diversified by 'artificial' selection into different varieties or breeds, some believers claim that it cannot happen to the degree that results in an entirely new species. Those people have shifted their stance from 'change doesn't happen at all' to 'change happens a little bit but not a lot'! They are accepting 'mini' evolution, as are those who have an annual flu vaccine. There is no reason to distinguish between 'small' evolution and 'big' evolution – that is a fabrication to suit creationists.

The other problem many believers have is accepting that change can happen naturally. They may have accepted 'artificial' selection but they ask themselves, since, as they believe, god created everything perfect to live on his Earth, *why would creatures need to change?* When the struggle for existence is pointed out to them, they start to admit that *adaptation,* as they prefer to call it, might be acceptable. Those people have shifted their stance from '*natural* selection doesn't happen at all' to '*natural* selection happens a little bit but not a lot'! They are accepting 'mini' natural selection. Again, there is no reason to imagine a boundary between 'little' bits of natural selection and 'big' bits. Where would you put this 'boundary'?

These are problems of *cognitive dissonance* for them; the evidence is in conflict with their childhood indoctrination and they have to make uncomfortable decisions. If only children weren't born to religious parents!

The Mechanism of Evolution
Some have a rather naïve idea of 'survival of the fittest'. The expression doesn't mean 'fit' in the sense

of spending time at the health club, which is the usual connotation of 'fit' in ordinary conversation. In evolutionary terms, 'fittest' refers to the individuals best adapted to occupy their niche in the environment; it *may* be the strongest, but equally it might mean the most disease resistant, the best camouflaged, the one with the sharpest eyesight or the most adaptable to change.

Many religious people completely fail to understand how evolution works. For a start, being hidebound in their religious way of thinking, they imagine that the universe and all the creatures in it have a purpose to fulfil – 'god's plan'. When they apply this style of thinking to the notion of evolution, they imagine that their 'Great Designer' must have started with simple things first (plants on the third day) and graduated to more complicated creatures later (fish on day five and land animals on day six). So they presuppose that evolution is driven by a need to develop in that way, from simple to sophisticated. *It isn't.*

Imagining a 'purpose' for creatures to fulfil is an example of *anthropomorphism:* seeing things through men's eyes and assuming that they are like us. Even commentators are guilty of this when they say something like, "The Queen must be feeling miserable in this rain" – how do they know how the Queen feels?

The only purpose that we know creatures to have is a biological one – to reproduce in an attempt to ensure the continuation of their species. This does not mean our lives are futile – see Chapter 11.

Evolution is not driven by purpose; it's driven by environmental pressures – changes in the habitat. These select the individuals that are most fit for the new conditions. For example, if the climate changes and the lake almost dries up, the fish will be under pressure to evolve into forms that can survive in the muddy bottom. If the lake overflows and the fish are washed into a dark cavern, different pressures will affect them – eyes will be vulnerable to damage for example.

Overall, life *has* evolved from simple organisms to complex ones as can be seen from the fossil record but, that's not happened 'on purpose'. Sometimes pressures may push in a direction that is opposite to the believers' 'progressive' direction and 'advanced' features may be lost. This explains how vestigial limb bones can be found in whales and snakes: their ancestors were limbed animals. This also explains the vestigial eyes of blind cave fish and the featureless bodies of intestinal parasites. The word 'devolution' has sometimes been applied to this phenomenon but it's a bad term because it incorporates the incorrect notion that it is going against the 'intended' direction towards increasing complexity when in reality there is no intended direction. We should never say that creatures evolve to become more advanced. *They don't.* They evolve to become better adapted to their environment, especially if it changes. There is no intended direction and no mysterious purpose.

The other big problem many believers have is with how organisms respond to these environmental pressures; *how is change brought about?* Well, given that the pressures apply to a *population* and individuals in a population show variation in every characteristic, some will be better adapted to survive and breed than others. How does that variation come about? This is where some believers mockingly cry *'random chance'!* I grant that evolution would be a vanishingly remote possibility if all of the features of a new species had to be derived by multiple throws of a dice. *But they are not!*

Perhaps at the beginning, when life was barely more than a molecule and there was no ozone layer to protect Earth's surface from mutagenic rays, mutation did play a large part, but it doesn't now. By far the most variation comes from *recombination;* organisms have such a large catalogue of genes that massive variation can be derived from shuffling them or from breaking them up and reassembling them. We didn't breed all those different dogs, from Dachshunds to great Danes, by mutating them! What would the Royal Society for the Prevention of Cruelty to Animals have had to say!

The cells of sexual organisms have two copies of every gene; they got one set from their father and one from their mother. When they reproduce, the chromosomes bearing these genes have to be reduced by half to make their sex cells – sperms and eggs. The nucleus in each cell of the egg-making or sperm-making tissue has to undergo a *reduction division;* during this process the chromosomes get tangled up and they exchange bits. They also get teamed up with some of the chromosomes from the other parental set so that the sperm or egg carries a novel mix of instructions not exactly the same as the parent or the grandparent; this is why we resemble our parents but are not identical to them. These shufflings, breakages and rejoinings produce many new characteristics without any need for mutation; it's like ripping up all the books in a library and pasting them back together inexactly.

So thousands of sperms, all different, meet up with eggs that are all different, which is *another opportunity for recombination,* and produce offspring that are all different. Hopefully, some of the variants will possess the qualities needed to respond to the environmental changes; if none do, the species will become extinct.

This is Natural Selection; it's the same process as dog-breeding but it is done by nature not by man.

How does it differ from Random Chance? Here's how: If you had 10 dice and you wanted to throw all sixes in one go, that would occur with a probability of once in 6,466,176 throws by random chance. However, if you were prepared to accept little improving steps towards your goal you would remove (select) the sixes from each throw and throw the rest again – you would get ten sixes quite soon that way. One die has six faces with one of them a six, so for ten dice there are 60 faces with 10 of them sixes – that's a 1 in 6 chance of getting one six. You might even get two sixes the first time you throw them all, then you would take out the ones that have come up six and throw the remaining nine or eight, which still have a 1:6 chance of one sixing. Each throw, the chance never goes above the 1 in 6 of the last die left. That's selection. If anyone talks to you about evolution being like random chance, what they are actually saying is, "I don't understand selection or probability".

Sometimes a group, part of a population, may be driven to migrate and may become isolated by a new river or mountain range so they can't breed with the original population. That would enable them to change differently and become a new species. If we separated

Great Danes from Dachshunds they might become non-fertile to one another; they are probably physically incompatible already! Separated groups gradually become non-fertile to each other and would then be called different 'species' (a manmade category). Lions and tigers are not completely non-fertile with each other yet – we can breed them in zoos; they are two *geographical* species who simply don't meet in the wild because the Indian Ocean is in the way! They are still evolving into pure species (using man's artificial definition of the word).

Yes, there may be the odd mutation occasionally tossed into the mix, but the process is much more like dealing cards and, in this game, the cards can be torn up and stuck to other torn pieces. Variation is almost entirely due to the recombination of existing information not the spontaneous introduction of mutated factors; indeed, most mutations prove to be fatal during development.

The Evidence for Evolution
EVIDENCE FROM FOSSILS
Some believers love to crow about 'missing links' or how, according to them, the Earth is only a few thousand years old. There is even a Creation Museum in Kentucky that features exhibits claiming to support the Genesis account. Much education is required here;

I have to explain a lot of geology before I can start on evolution itself.

Firstly, let's state the Creationists' position. Jews, Muslims and Christians claim that, in the beginning, god created the universe in one week. Remember, as reported in Genesis, he said, 'Let there be light' on the first day, made the heavens on the second day, made dry land and plants on the third day, named the day and the night on the fourth day, made sea creatures and birds on the fifth day and land animals on the sixth day.

There are several problems with that account. For a start, we cannot be sure what the bible authors meant by 'sea creatures' and by 'animals'. Scientists find those words a bit vague but would probably take 'creatures' to mean all organisms including plants, and 'animals' to mean all organisms that are *not* plants or fungi or bacteria. So birds, humans and many 'sea creatures' are all animals even though we are told they were created on different days. What can the bible mean? It's just confusing!

Then there is the timescale; we haven't discovered all the species yet so we're not sure how many there are in total but, just taking beetles as a sample group (*one which was not mentioned in the bible incidentally – not in the creation story nor in Noah's flood, unless you count Leviticus 11:22, which actually refers to locusts – Ornithopterans not Coleopterans),* we have identified over 350,000 different beetle species currently living, not counting all the extinct ones! (Compare that to the mere 5000 different mammals, almost a quarter of them bats!) It was a big job creating all those organisms in parts of four days, wasn't it!

> "God seems to have an inordinate fondness for beetles."
> **J. B. S. Haldane**

Christian apologists claim that the biblical 'day' may have been a longer unit of time – do you hear the sound of a barrel being scraped? In fact, our planet's day *has* changed but it's got *longer* than when Earth was young, not shorter; computer simulations indicate the primordial day was only about six hours long! The rotation rate has been slowing due to the drag of the moon. That's why we have to insert 'leap seconds' into the day every so often.

In the 17th century, the Archbishop of Armagh and Primate of all Ireland, James Ussher, calculated from his literal reading of the bible that creation began at 9am on October 23rd, 4004 BC! That day was a Sunday so, if the Archbishop was right, the seventh day of rest would be a Saturday – Jews celebrate the correct day, Christians (Sunday) and Muslims (Friday) have got it 'wrong'! Even allowing for the changes to calendars over the centuries, this is the sort of disagreement that makes the whole story sound implausible, surely!

Fossils were discovered by Aristotle on a mountain top and he observed that they resembled the seashells found on a beach. At the time, this was a puzzle because the mountain looked too solid to have popped up of its own accord and it was a long way down to the sea.

We now know that land *moves*. Not just the molten stuff that erupts from a volcano, but solid rock moves too, albeit very slowly. Earth's land masses are like the skin on custard! It's a crust that 'floats' on Earth's under-layer, the semi-molten rock of the 'mantle'. Over the billennia the crust has broken up into 'tectonic plates' that have floated about and bashed together. When that happens, the colliding surfaces can be buckled up into ripples – these are mountain ranges. Aristotle's fossils were once on the seabed but now, the former seabed is a mountain top.

Before we can proceed much further with this, we need to go over some geology, so here goes:

The scripture writers didn't know that our planet's core has two layers and the outer one is a very hot liquid under pressure at between 4000 and 6000 degrees Centigrade; or that this heat sets up convection currents in the 'mantle' the semi molten material between the core and the crust. There are three types of rock in the crust, classified according to how they were formed.

Igneous rock comes from 'magma' – semi-molten toffee-like rock that rises on convection currents in the mantle. If it is pushed up beneath the surface it *intrudes* into the crust and solidifies into a dykes, sills or huge slabs called batholiths which cover vast areas of our planet's surface such as Scotland and most of Africa. It is usually hard so it erodes slowly forming thin soil but may contain seams of gold or diamonds. If it is pushed up more vigorously, it *extrudes* through volcanoes as molten lava and cools down quickly. This includes pumice, solidified foam which is formed from gaseous lava. Igneous rocks have no fossils.

Sedimentary rock comes from the erosion of the crust into particles by the forces of weather including sunshine (which causes expansion and, at night, contraction making rock shatter), rain (which dissolves soluble minerals and freezes into ice that wedges crevices apart) and wind, which abrades surfaces with the sharp, hard particles it blows along. Other forces include glaciers, which scour the surface, and rivers, which cut valleys and wash all this eroded material into the sea where it sinks to the bottom as sediment and hardens into rock.

Sediment arrives chronologically; the oldest material is at the bottom and, as different materials turn up at different times, they form layers (strata) like a multidecker sandwich. There are plenty of places where you can observe this stratification: cliffs and canyons are good. We can work out the rough age of a layer according to where it is in the order – the oldest is usually at the bottom, although much better dating can be done using radiometric methods. All sorts of stuff can form sedimentary rock, it just depends what gets in the water and sinks – particles of sand and clay, seashells, rotting vegetation, insects' exoskeletons, vertebrates' skeletons, etc. It all gets compressed under the weight of the upper layers and the water above it and hardens into rock over the millennia. This is the type of rock that contains fossils and, when earth movements bring sedimentary rocks to the surface, we might find them.

Metamorphic rock is sedimentary rock that has been heated and compressed. How does this happen? Well, you remember that the pieces of crust collide?

Sometimes, when they bang together, one edge buckles downwards and goes under the other into the hot mantle where it gets cooked and changed, chalk turns into marble, for example. Any fossils that might have been in the original rock usually get ruined.

Rock Dating. Rocks can be pretty accurately dated using radiometric methods; this is based on the fact that some elements undergo radioactive decay over extremely long periods of many millions of years. In a rock, these elements can be trapped *with* their decay products so it's just a matter of quantifying their relative proportions and then reading off from a graph how much time must have passed since the rock was formed.
See: www.youtube.com/watch?v=phZeE7Att_s

As you may have gathered, the likelihood of anything becoming a fossil is pretty remote. A complicated set of circumstances has to be met. Firstly, a creature must have hard parts that resist decay – very little soft material survives the process of fossilization unless it is frozen or surrounded by tar or resin. Secondly, its body must end up in water – this is much more likely for aquatic organisms than land based ones. Thirdly, it usually needs to be 'petrified (turned to stone) in order to resist the forces it will encounter over the length of time it takes for sedimentary rock to form. Fourthly, an earth movement has to occur to force that stratum to the surface and turn that piece of seabed into land. Fifthly, erosion needs to take place to expose the layers which may look promising to a geologist and, sixthly, someone has to discover it and recognise it as a fossil! *What are the chances of all that happening?*

No wonder, in the early days of palaeontology, there were many gaps in the fossil record. Since the discipline began in 1800 though, many millions of fossils have been added to the record and many of the gaps have been filled in. For example, there is a gap-free fossil record for the evolution of the horse. Sadly, most believers are not up to speed with the latest facts and, while they get their information from biased sources, like the Creation Museum, they won't be.

If you encounter anyone claiming that there are too many 'missing links' for evolution to be true, direct them to Wikipedia:
http://en.m.wikipedia.org/List_of_transitional_fossils

Ever wondered why nobody questions the 'missing links' in faith, like the leap required to go from, for example, 'the bible is true' to 'there is a supernatural creator'? Is it because of the elephant in the room syndrome?

I don't want to make this into a textbook because there are plenty of websites you can visit to study fossils, just be sure that they are not creationist ones! Suffice it to say that the evidence indicates the world is about 4.6 billion years old, life began about 4 billion years ago with very simple life forms and, for the most part, has become increasingly complex as time has passed. This doesn't fit the proposition that all the creatures were created 'perfect' in four days a mere six thousand years ago, but it does fit well with Darwin's Theory of Evolution by Natural Selection.

EVIDENCE FROM ANATOMY

Anatomical structures often serve different purposes and, if they were created perfect, you might expect them to be designed from scratch for the job in question in the same way that men have designed boats, cars and aircraft to suit their functions. *Not a bit of it!* They are often *homologous:* developed on the same platform. *Why would a designer god do that?*

Take the forelimbs of tetrapods (vertebrates with limbs), for example. The flipper of a seal, the wing of a bird, the front leg of a newt, the wing of a bat, and the fore limb of a rabbit all have one bone in the upper limb, two bones in the lower limb, a collection of small bones in the wrist and five digits in the paw. Sometimes a few small bones have been lost or become fused together and they may vary in length, but they are all based on the same pattern – the 'pentadactyl limb'. *Is this a coincidence, is god trying to trick us, or have they evolved from a common ancestor?* You choose.

Then there is the question of 'perfection'. Take the giraffe's recurrent laryngeal nerve for example; it travels down the giraffe's long neck from the larynx, takes a U turn under the aortic arch in the chest and the heads back up again to get to the brain! *Would anyone with any sense have designed it like that?* No, that would be *imperfection!* But when you realise that the laryngeal nerve originated in fish, which *have no neck*, the penny drops – it's evidence for evolution!

Similarly, who would design the retina of the mammalian eye with the nerves on top, casting shadows on the light sensitive layer? When men design digital cameras, they sensibly put the wires out of the back!

CELLULAR/MOLECULAR EVIDENCE
Microscopic evidence for evolution has come a long way in the last hundred years and makes a powerful contribution to the evidence that was available in Darwin's day. The more we discover of the fine structure of organisms, the more similarities appear.

Early microscopists noticed that all creatures are made of cells and almost every cell contains a nucleus. More recently, electron microscopes have enabled the detection of two other omnipresent cellular organelles, mitochondria and ribosomes and centrifugal fractionation has shown that all cellular organisms have DNA as their genetic material. The ubiquitous nature of these components is an obvious example of common ancestry.

Our recently acquired ability to read the genetic code on the DNA has uncovered facts such as the percentage of genes we humans share with other species: Bacteria share 7% with us, Mustard Cress 15%, Roundworms 21%, Fruit fly 36%, Zebra Fish 85%, Chimpanzee 98%. Notice that the closer you get to human anatomy, the greater the genetic similarity. The best explanation for such progressive commonality is that organisms share a 'family tree' with branches coming off an ancestral 'trunk'; in other words, we have evolved.

Most recently, a new branch of genetics has opened up – Epigenetics. This studies the modification of the message on the DNA when it is transcribed and translated during protein synthesis; it reveals that factors inherited in the genome can be amplified or suppressed on their way to becoming expressed as characteristics. This mechanism shows that the environment can exert an influence on an organism even during its lifetime. If a starving mouse is suddenly allowed access to unlimited food they will overfeed and become obese. Puzzlingly, their pups and grand-pups will inherit the tendency for obesity too! The 'Nature versus Nurture' debate has just got much more complicated! Further research is needed.

GEOGRAPHICAL EVIDENCE

The distribution of organisms around the globe illustrates how some have evolved in isolation. Evidence obtained by matching rock formations that are currently separated by oceans, using radiometry and magnetism, indicate that Earth's continents were united into one land mass back in the Jurassic era. Gondwanaland, as it is called, has subsequently split into fragments of crust and migrated to form the current map. It's not a coincidence that the East coast of South America looks as if it would fit like a piece of jigsaw puzzle into the West coast of Africa; it really did!

When you consider the populations of mammals in Australia, South Africa and South America, you find that they have distinct types – including marsupials that are not found in Europe, Africa, Asia or North America. *Did god make them that way or have they evolved differently because their homelands separated thousands of years ago, preventing them from interbreeding with their ancestors?*

Volcanic island populations are particularly interesting because they rose out of the sea above their chains of volcanoes relatively recently in the geological timescale. Only species capable of migrating from the mainland or of getting windblown on tangles of floating vegetation could colonise them. This isolation has led to evolutionary diversification of ancestrally related species due to the different environmental pressures on their individual islands. The variety of beak adaptations, driven by dietary opportunities, shown by the finches on the Galapagos Islands was what prompted Darwin to ponder natural selection.

So, there is plenty of convincing evidence to support the Theory of Evolution by Natural Selection; that's why it has gained such wide acceptance in thinking circles. Before I leave this chapter, however, I wish to put the lie to a typically erroneous claim made by believers; that the human eye is too complex to have evolved and, therefore, must have been created. They state: buildings are designed, aircraft are too, paintings, watches and computers, all complicated things have a designer. *Well, yes they do, all manmade things have been designed in a sense, but what's that got to do with anything? Do you claim that, because birds are known to build nests, mice and gorillas must have employed birds to build their nests? What about the White Cliffs of Dover? The Grand Canyon? Who designed them? Don't some things happen by natural processes? Can god really be controlling every eroding molecule of water?*

The creationist argue for 'irreducible complexity' – the notion that a nomad who discovers a watch in the desert would rightfully assume that it was so complex that it must have been made. Please note, he hasn't *found* a watchmaker, he has merely *assumed* one.

Anyone studying the evolution of vision soon notices that it begins in single celled organisms with the possession of a molecule that detects light thereby enabling the creature to swim towards brightness for photosynthesis opportunities. Later, multicellular organisms develop a hemispherical depression lined with cells containing this molecule (rhodopsin); that bowl shaped organ enables the recognition of shadows. Continuing along the timescale, the dent closes up except for a small hole – that is a pinhole camera that can form images. Finally, a lens evolved and the eye was fully developed. This process has happened several times – insect eyes, octopus eyes, and mammalian eyes. This is the nutshell version – search online for more information.

Summary

Evolution is not a theory, but a *Theory* – a scientific model of the natural world that fits the evidence and enables predictions that can be tested for validity. There is plenty of convincing evidence to support it. It has become accepted by almost all scientists, the Roman Catholic Church, the Church of England and, in well educated societies, a majority of the general public. In the twenty-first century, denying evolution is tantamount to saying, "Fire does not burn".

To those who assert that Evolution requires faith, I say, *"Faith is a belief on steroids; it is an unquestioned belief. How does not questioning something make it stronger? Why would an Evolutionist want this faith stuff?"*

Here is the argument for evolution in a nutshell:

1. Are you identical to your mother and father?
   No = acceptance of variation.
2. Do you accept that we have bred many different varieties of dog?
   Yes = acceptance of 'artificial' selection.
3. Do you accept that there are pressures in the environment such as predators, diseases, famines and floods?
   Yes = acceptance of struggle for existence.

4. Do you accept that we need to develop a new flu vaccine every year because the virus has changed into a form that is better at beating off last year's vaccination?

    Yes = acceptance of natural selection ('micro-evolution') and survival of the fittest.

5. So, could you explain how, given enough time, the small adaptations that you accept *do* happen, would be prevented from accumulating into enough differences to be described as a new species?

    No = acceptance of speciation.

Please note, the Theory of Evolution does not demand speciation, only creationists do that. There is no scientific reason to distinguish between 'micro-evolution' and 'macro-evolution'. Where would you put such a boundary? Why not 'middle-sized evolution'?!

Please also note that evolution is not motivated by a desire for progress towards complexity or advancement. When people ask you, *"If we come from apes, why do apes still exist?"* they are revealing their misunderstanding. Apes are good at their jobs – they fit their environment, that's why they are still successful. They will continue to succeed unless we compete them out of their habitat by felling rainforests. The same applies to worms.

By the way, we do not come from present day apes, humans and apes share a common ancestor, which is extinct, in the same way that you did not come from your cousin but you share a great, great, grandfather, who is also extinct!

"We must question the story logic of having an all-knowing, all powerful God, who creates faulty humans then blames them for his own mistakes!"
Gene Roddenberry

"The man who says 'Believe as I do or god will damn you, will presently say, believe as I do or I shall assassinate you'."
Voltaire

9. MORALITY and FORGIVENESS

We are taught in houses of worship that morality comes from the 'Scriptures' (that word just means 'writings'):

- Christians claim that 'God' handed down 'commandments' on 'tablets' to Moses on Mount Sinai. And that Jesus also set out some rules in the 'Sermon on the Mount'.

- Islam, being an Abrahamic religion, accepts the Old Testament of the Bible but does not consider it to be the word of god. Various moral principles are presented throughout the Qu'ran, some 'voiced' by the Prophet Muhammad and some by 'Allah' himself.

- Jews have 613 'mitzvot' (commandments) listed in The Old Testament of the Bible and the Torah.

- Hinduism is all about 'finding peace' and it has Yamas and Niyamas, which have a rough equivalence to the Christian Commandments.

- Buddhism has 'Ten Courses of Unwholesome Action' including: Eat temperately and not at all in the afternoons. Do not watch dancing, nor listen to singing or plays! Wear no garlands, perfumes or any adornments. Sleep not in luxurious beds! Accept no gold or silver!

You might think that, without these instructions on how to behave, we humans would be a barbaric lot! That, of course, is what the religious leaders want us to think. They want to be able to prey on your conscience and threaten 'retribution' (godly punishment) unless you do as they say and they promise 'salvation' if you attend their church (and make donations), make confessions (and a donation) and submit to their control. They don't want to lose you from their 'flock'; *where would their next meal come from?*

The truth is very different. We are social animals and all social animals have evolved co-operative behaviours. See:
http://www.ted.com/talks/lang/en/frans_de_waal_do_animals_have_morals.html

Do you think that the apes, monkeys and elephants in that video have read the Bible or the Koran to get their morals?

If you *do* read the Bible (and don't forget, three large religions are based on the Old Testament), you will find some horrifying morality. It exemplifies war, misogyny, homophobia, killing the first-born, slavery, gruesome punishments, forcing daughters to marry their rapists and stoning disobedient children to death!

Although there is incomplete agreement between Roman Catholic and Protestant versions, four of the ten Christian 'commandments' are about *worship*, that is, about protecting or safeguarding the religion itself (early priests were obviously paranoid):
1. I am the LORD thy god, thou shalt have no other god but me,
2. Thou shalt have no graven images or likenesses,
3. Thou shalt not take the LORD's name in vain,
4. Thou shalt remember the Sabbath day.

The first one is just an assertion and the next three are exhortations to submit to the religious hierarchy; we have to get to number five before we find any useful advice for citizens of an orderly society:
5. Honour thy father and mother,

And to number six before we get to a proper law –
6. Thou shalt not kill,
7. Thou shalt not commit adultery,
8. Thou shalt not steal,
9. Thou shalt not bear false witness,
10. Thou shalt not covet. (Source: Wikipedia)

Please notice that rape is not mentioned! Neither is assault! The commandments were obviously written by men, for men, in a male dominated society! The Qur'an is the same – it promises men an afterlife with 72 virgins in a paradise flowing with wine, and nothing for women! Misogyny rules in the monotheisms! You must have noticed that there are still no female Anglican bishops or Roman Catholic priests.

Assuming the commandments were put in order of importance, it is obvious that the authors were much more interested in securing their incomes and privileged positions in society than in outlawing theft and murder, let alone rape and assault! *Do you really want to make the bible your moral compass?*

Christians will often claim that unpalatable verses are 'taken out of context' or should be read as appropriate for the historic times in which the texts were set. *Does that sound like excuses to you? Are they cherry picking just the bits of the Bible they like?* Especially as, in the next breath, some will claim the Bible is God's word and should be taken literally!

Or they may claim that Christ came and rendered the Old Testament redundant. The difficulty with that is, according to the New Testament, Jesus stated that he endorsed the early scriptures and you can find inappropriate antisocial advice in the NT too!

Anyone who thinks that empathy, love, compassion, devotion, sympathy, co-operation and loyalty are exclusively human traits cannot have had a dog! A pet dog knows when we are sick and mourns with us when we grieve. My brother-in-law recounts how, when he was a boy, they had two dogs; one got killed on the road and the other one cried all night. *Can you tell a story of your dog showing its feelings?*

Those characteristics are the necessary precursors to a moral society. That's why dogs are man's best friend, but all social animals have rules to live by – that's how they keep their society calm and stable. Moral behaviour has evolved. It doesn't come from ancient religious books so it doesn't belong to priests; we can do without their sermons about fear and 'salvation'!

In order to trick us into thinking we need their Bible to 'be good', Christians have invented the concept of 'Original Sin'. This claims that, thanks to Adam's rib woman, Eve, eating the fruit shown to her by the talking snake in the Garden of Eden, all babies are born with 'sin' already implanted in their bodies! Or are they trying to scare us into wanting their 'salvation'; an imaginary solution to an imaginary threat! To receive 'salvation' you are expected to give them money! *Why does that remind me of a gangster protection racket?*

Behaviour that is done for a reward, such as forgiveness or salvation, is like prostitution isn't it? Payment takes away the morality.

Forgiveness is a Good Idea, Isn't it?
Well, yes it is, we need to release criminals from their crimes, after completing their punishment, in order to reduce the rate of recidivism. It's such a good idea the Catholic Church has assumed ownership of it and turned it into a commercial business! Money equals power (and power corrupts).

Centuries ago, you could buy a 'Papal Dispensation' to 'wash away your sins'! It was an official looking document with a Papal seal and signature. King Henry VIIIth bought one so that he could be permitted to marry his first wife, who was a widow and needed to have her first marriage dissolved. Her husband's death was not enough to make her available because the church saw an opportunity for earning! (Subsequently, Henry's conflicts with Rome resulted in him forming the Church of England.)

Later Popes started giving away free 'Dispensations' to those who travelled to Rome and pledged their obedience to the church. They realised that members of their flock who were prepared to make the commitment required to undergo a long journey were acting like unpaid ambassadors for the faith and they would probably make generous donations, while they were around, with no need for coercion.

Catholic Priests still offer 'absolution' in the confessional for the price of a minor punishment in the form of expressions of loyalty to the faith: Hail Mary prayers. *What's wrong with that you may ask?* Well, if you can cast off your bad deeds and become 'clean' again, you are being released from responsibility for your actions on Earth. It's a bit like James Bond's 'Licence to kill'!

In April 2011, a Brazilian gunman killed twelve schoolchildren then shot himself; his suicide note revealed that he expected to be forgiven! *Do we really want members of society to have church permits to be irresponsible?* Especially now that it turns out the Roman Catholic clergy were absolving each other from child abuse!

That episode has adversely affected recruitment to the priesthood and membership of the Catholic Church but, strangely, had no affect on Tony Blair who crossed over from Anglicanism none-the-less! At a book signing in Dublin in September 2010, the former UK PM was pelted with eggs, bottles and shoes by anti-war protestors expressing disapproval of what they consider to have been an illegal invasion of Iraq instigated with 'born again' USA President George W Bush in 2003. *Should we beware of electing to power men who have certainty that their 'Lord' is backing their actions? Are doubters safer?*

Should you Endorse Religious Crimes?
If your football supporters' club started fighting with the arch rival club and someone died, what would you do?
I'll tell you what I would do: I'd resign. There is no way I'd want to belong to a club whose members did that. Belonging means accepting, condoning and sharing responsibility for the group's behaviour; even moderate members are complicit; silence is collusion. If you make donations to your faith you may even be inadvertently sponsoring fundamentalist activity!

Some religious people are waking up to this and distancing themselves from 'organised' religion because they don't agree with some of its members' activities or the more damaging parts of its 'creed'. They effectively start a little religion of their own.

Sadly, some of these people are charismatic leaders and their little religion grows into a cult like the 'Branch

Davidians', 82 of whom died in fires at a siege of their premises at Waco in Texas in 1993. Several cult mass suicides have occurred, see link:
http://en.wikipedia.org/wiki/Cult_suicides

This phenomenon illustrates how innocent, ignorant and desperate people are extremely vulnerable to falling into the trap of religion. An exceptional leader can amass a flock of followers willing to sacrifice their own lives for him and his false promises. Humans are social animals and, like all social animals, we have evolved to be led by a leader. We are primates and we have our equivalent of silverback gorillas in our societies. The leader keeps control, reducing conflict between rivals which increases the likelihood of reproductive success and, therefore, the continuation of the species.

Recent research has discovered a correlation between strong faith and religious strife; communities such as in Northern Ireland and Israel live in ghettoes demarcated by high walls in an attempt to keep the peace.

There is also a strong negative correlation between the level of scientific education of a society and its religious fervour. In Western Europe and the US East and West coasts, where many have higher education, secular opinions prevail. Scientifically educated people are less easily led. Nowadays less than 3% of the UK population regularly go to church.

It is conditions of desperation and ignorance that enable religions to thrive. Some societies even believe you can see the future in a set of goat's entrails (guts)! *Why would you join the ignorant?*

Summary

Religions have appropriated morality and forgiveness as theirs to dispense. We must demand these social concepts back!

I contend that it is immoral to believe. Non-belief has the moral high ground: no-one kills in the name of no god. Indeed, failing to actively campaign for the elimination of the scourge of religion is also immoral; it should be our moral duty to stop the religious circumcision of infants without their consent, for example.

> *"Men never commit evil so fully and joyfully as when they do it for religious convictions."*
> **Blaise Pascal**

10. HEAVEN, SIN and HELL

There are many 'Heavens'!
Jews have seven; it's a hierarchy. The first one is the entry level and the seventh heaven is the most sublime; hence the expression, *'to be in Seventh Heaven'*.

In Norse paganistic mythology, heaven is known as 'Valhalla', which is described as an enormous majestic hall ruled over by the god Odin. 'Nirvana' is the heaven for both Buddhism and Jainism. To enter the Ancient Egyptian Heaven you had to pass through the 'Underworld' in a quest called the Duat. There are many more tales of 'Heavens'.

Like all good clubs though, 'Heaven' has entry conditions; you won't get a look in at any heaven unless you have joined the appropriate sect in advance. Even then you have to be well behaved because, according to the legends, you will only be admitted to heaven by the 'grace of god', whatever that is. Fortunately, it's never too late to sign up – deathbed conversions have always been popular! For those of us who can't make the grade, there are mythical dystopias to end up in such as purgatory, limbo and hell.

'Sins' are the supposedly naughty acts which aggregate into 'evil', the concept of an overarching 'badness' that is the prerogative of the 'devil' called 'Satan'. *It's all rubbish!* There is no evidence for the existence of any of those ideas. These are the tools of priests and, often, their ruling sponsors, used for keeping a population under control. If you can frighten your congregation or your subjects into behaving 'righteously' so that their 'souls' might go to 'heaven' and enjoy everlasting bliss, you can more easily retain your superior social status and save a fortune in state security!

These notions made Christianity into a powerful force for British colonisers of West Africa. Armed trading ships opened the way, followed by missionaries soon afterwards who, possibly unintentionally, subdued the native population with promises of salvation to 'heaven' if they were 'righteous', which was taken by the locals to mean accepting of the white man's authority.

The truth is all social animals have evolved standards of acceptable behaviour. We do not need to fall for the guilt trips that the priests try to impose upon us.

The Dangers of Heaven
The desire to go to a better place might be construed as giving us a reason to behave 'righteously' during our

earthly existence but it can also be interpreted in exactly the opposite way. *'How can heaven be dangerous?'* I hear you ask.

Well, if you wish to cut short your human body form and achieve your magnificent spiritual survival early by becoming a 'martyr', you might be prepared to slaughter several members of other religions! Such a massacre would be perfectly moral of course because your god would be on your side! This was at least part of the motivation behind what Americans call 9/11 (the attack on the World Trade Centre towers in New York on 11/09/2001); the Islamic fundamentalist suicide pilots were each assured of an eternal existence with seventy two virgins in heaven.

Why would you hang around on Earth if you could get killed whilst doing your god's work, become a 'martyr', and get to heavenly, virgin filled, paradise sooner?

Why 'Heaven'?
Well, life on Earth is stressful. Whether we're in a poor country wondering if we have the strength to fetch water or in a rich nation struggling to pay the bills, we all have pressures upon us. That's why the vision of achieving a safe and peaceful ending is such an appealing concept; it meets a psychological need.

Fairy tales encapsulate this idea in the phrase, *"and they all lived happily ever after"*.

It's the stresses of life and the possibility that they might be resolved by entry to heaven that gives us the notion of *'Salvation'*. Being *'saved'* from a 'hell' even worse than your daily existence, is a particularly attractive prospect if you live in a deprived community; it's much better than being dead! 'Salvation' also gives priests something to promise and someone to talk about – the *'Saviour'*.

The concept of 'heaven' is a great tool for those in power. If a ruler can convince the masses that they have an idyllic existence to look forward to in the future, they are more likely to be content and meek and obedient in the here and now. That's why states often reward religious leaders: in the UK, 26 Bishops are given a seat in the House of Lords with an attendance allowance: £300 ($480) a day tax-free + expenses!

So, if you subscribe to the proposition of heaven you are signing up to the continuation of your society's current authority. *Isn't that something to bear in mind if you are being oppressed by a dictatorial despot or a corrupt government?*

Stairway to 'Heaven'?

Well, where is it? Historically, it was pictured in the clouds, but we have not detected it yet despite searching at all wavelengths of the electromagnetic spectrum and being able to see more than 13 billion light years into the distance! Some say it has retreated to being *'within us'; do they mean in our imagination?*

Hell

All religions seem to have come up with the concept of a 'hell'. It's the stick to go with the carrot of 'heaven'. Over the centuries the description of 'hell' has got worse; it's now a fiery place where your 'soul' is tortured throughout eternity.

Christian children are borne with 'original sin' (thanks to Eve eating the 'forbidden fruit') and would have to suffer this burning fate if they die before being 'baptised', according to early doctrine. Hundreds of years ago, perceiving the grief that this would cause the parents of deceased new born babies, the leaders of the Roman Catholic Church came up with 'limbo' – a painless place for the 'souls' of these innocents to end up in for ever! In April 2007, Pope Benedict XVI abolished 'limbo' saying the unbaptised children should be allowed into heaven to enjoy the 'beatific vision'. *That was generous of him, wasn't it?!*

The Pope's action indicates two things:

1. That 'limbo' was a hypothesis – an invention of men which can be abandoned when it becomes unpopular. Benedict even acknowledged, "Limbo was just a theological concept after all." That entitles us to wonder how much else the priests have made up.

2. That maybe there is a problem with the morality of the hell concept: *why should the 'souls' of good men get tortured for eternity just because they haven't had the opportunity, or chosen, to worship the 'right' god?*

Summary

The concepts of 'heaven', 'hell', 'souls', the 'devil', 'angels', 'cherubs', etc. have no supporting evidence for their existence. 'Limbo' has already been exposed as only a 'theological concept' and has been abandoned by the Catholic Church. *What will go next? Virgin birth? Resurrection? Walking on water? Water into wine?* All of those things have been claimed for several gods before Jesus. Keep an eye open for future developments!

Wheelchair users can't go to heaven – apparently there's only a stairway!

11. THE CASE AGAINST RELIGION

How do you feel about the recent scandal in the UK involving horsemeat being passed off as beef? Outraged at the deception? So you should be!

Something similar happened in February 2011 that drew attention to *religious* deception: the UK Advertising Standards Authority banned advertisements by a group called 'Healing On The Streets' run by a consortium of 20 churches in Bath. Some volunteers had set up a stall outside Bath Abbey offering to pray for sick people. They gave out leaflets claiming 'GOD CAN HEAL TODAY!' and listing conditions suitable for their prayer 'cure': 'Back Pain, Arthritis, Muscular Sclerosis, Addiction, Cancer, Ulcers, Depression, Allergies, Fibromyalgia, Asthma, Paralysis, Crippling Diseases, Phobias, Sleeping Disorders, and *any other sickness*'!

The ASA said they had not seen people healed through these prayers, that the adverts could encourage false hope in sufferers and were therefore irresponsible. They banned them saying the organisation must not make claims which stated or implied that, by receiving prayer from these volunteers, people could be healed of medical conditions. So, it's official! Religions are trying to scam us!

In a more recent court case, the judge told the court, "In the eye of everyone save the believer, religious faith is necessarily subjective being incommunicable by any kind of proof or evidence."
See:

http://www.telegraph.co.uk/news/religion/7652358/Gary-McFarlane-judges-assault-on-irrational-religious-freedom-claims-in-sex-therapist-case.html

Sadly, many believers have lost their lives through their belief; in October 2011, the BBC reported that, in the UK, at least three people with HIV died soon after following the advice of priests to stop taking their medication and start praying. This is very common in countries where religion is taken more seriously.

Even in the USA, where you might hope for high standards of care, male infants die every year from circumcision. *Do we need circumcision?* There are no proven benefits; it's genital mutilation and, being done at that age, makes it child abuse.

One doesn't have to live long to notice that men do bad things for their gods. *Since there is no justification for any religion, shouldn't that be enough reason to* abandon faiths? *I don't need to write a chapter on 'The Case against Fairies', do I?* People do not seriously believe in them or commit atrocities for Tinker Bell. In that respect, fairies are better than god!

The Defence of the Faith

Religions often purport to be good and peaceful but, unfortunately, the practice differs from the theory. Like all organisations, religions serve a purpose; they provide a service: that of looking after the 'spiritual' needs of society. Again, like all human groupings, religions have a hierarchical structure – ranks of leadership, this means that the leaders determine policy and actions and enjoy the submission of their subordinates.

In the recent news item about Cardinal Keith O'Brien's resignation following his admission that his sexual conduct, "Had fallen beneath the standards expected of him", the priests who 'outed' him for importuning them revealed that they had taken thirty years to pluck up the courage because the Bishop had immense power over them, being able to control every aspect of their lives; church society is still feudal.

Since faith lacks foundation, these leaders feel insecure and one of the items at the top of their agenda is to continuously reinforce their position. This requires a lot of appearances and preaching to dogmatically repeat the assertions of their particular faith; it also requires managing a recruitment department, like the Alpha course, to increase membership – all religions, convinced in their rectitude, are ambitious to become the only religion in the world!

The outcome of these initiatives is to divide mankind into factions and the trouble with being in factions is our natural suspicion drives us in the direction of antagonism, fear and demonization. *Don't we have enough real divisions without a non-evidential one?*

Early English Kings claimed to have the power to rule given to them by God! This is called the 'Divine Right' of Kings. Not only that, but some of them had scribes prepare a family tree purporting to show that they had actually *descended* from God! They felt that entitled them to rule as cruelly as they liked. *What unbelievable arrogance!*

This need to defend the faith from criticism has led to the invention of the imaginary crimes of 'Heresy' – denying religious doctrine, 'Blasphemy' – offending the leaders of a religion, 'Sacrilege' – damaging the property of a religious organisation and 'Apostasy' – quitting a religion. Sadly, men have been imprisoned and executed for all of these 'offences'; in some countries, they are still being prosecuted. In an era of mostly democratic governments, we must ask, *why does an organisation need such harsh punishments to retain loyalty? Is it because the claims of religions are being perceived by better-educated folk as illegitimate?*

Atrocities committed 'In the name of The Lord'
'Born again' Christian, President George W Bush told Palestinian Ministers that God told him to invade Afghanistan and Iraq! Reported by the BBC, according to Palestinian Prime Minister Abu Mazen and his Foreign Minister, Nabil Shaath, President Bush said, *"I'm driven with a mission from God. God would tell me, 'George, go and fight those terrorists in Afghanistan.' And I did, and then God would tell me, 'George, go and end the tyranny in Iraq.'"*

Assisted by Catholic convert, UK Prime Minister Tony Blair, George W Bush invaded Iraq in 2003 and precipitated the death of over 300 British soldiers, over 5000 US soldiers and more than 106,000 Iraqi civilians. Perhaps, for men who have suspended their critical powers enough to believe in a god, it's an easy progression to presume that their actions are 'righteous'.

Of course, wars are usually fought for more than one reason – resources like oil are often a big factor, *but removing the 'justification' of a non-evidential 'god' being on your 'side' would be a big improvement, wouldn't it?*

In the Crusades or 'Holy' wars, fought in the 11th and 12th centuries, up to 9 million people were killed, half of them Christians. On a smaller scale, Peter Sutcliff, the 'Yorkshire Ripper', killed 13 prostitutes claiming that he was the tool of God's will; he is locked up.

If people realised that, based on the evidence, God is probably less likely to exist than the Loch Ness Monster, such atrocities might not happen. Nobody kills in the name of Nessie! Beware of men who are *certain* that they are backed by 'God'. Doubters are much more harmless!

The Language of the Lord

Like many specialisms, religions have their own jargon. Words like 'Shibboleth', 'Amen', 'Alleluia' (Hallelujah), 'Heresy', 'Fatwa', 'Jihad', 'Crusade', 'Intefada', 'Heathen', 'Blasphemy' and 'Apostasy' have little use in secular communications.

See next page for more about religious words:

A RELIGIOUS VOCABULARY

- Blasphemy: Irreverence toward holy personages.
- Heresy: Disagreeing with the doctrine of the church.
- Infidel: someone who does not belong to *your* religion.
- Crusade: Religiously sanctioned military campaign (Christian for Jihad).
- Fatwa: Ruling issued by an Islamic scholar.
- Jihad: Struggle or warfare for the expansion and defence of the Islamic state (Islamic for Crusade).
- Intefada: Uprising, resistance or rebellion.
- Shibboleth: Something that identifies a speaker as being a member of a religion (usually used to identify 'infidels').
- Heathen: someone who is not a member of *your/any* religion!

Do you notice that many of the words in the religious vocabulary are concerned with loyalty to your own group and hatred of others? This leads to fundamentalism, isn't that divisive?

Fundamental extremists commit atrocities in the 'Name of God'. *Do you want to tacitly condone their actions by supporting the same religion?*

I know what you'll say, "That's not religion's fault. It's evil men using religion as an excuse." That's similar to the position of the gun lobby – "Guns don't kill, men do." Well, guns sure make killing a lot easier. And religions provide a ready-made 'justification' and excuse for atrocities. *Have you ever heard of a suicide bomber doing it for atheism?* Let's remove one *unnecessary* reason for malicious acts.

Yes, any two groups of men can be stirred into antagonism towards each other; feelings can escalate into demonization and violence. Let's eliminate non-evidential reasons for forming gangs, we have enough real ones; *wouldn't it be better to have one hateful motivation less? Many faiths have already gone – does anyone fight over Zeus versus Thor?*

On September 1st 2009, The Telegraph conducted a survey of the top ten worst Bible passages, which indicate, in the minds of their readers, approval for sexism, genocide and slavery.

Here are the references:

No. 1: 1 Timothy 2:12:

"I do not permit a woman to teach or to have authority over a man; she must be silent."

This promotes sexual inequality and disrespect of half the population! Did men write this I wonder?

No. 2: 1 Samuel 15:3: *"This is what the Lord Almighty says... 'Now go and strike Amalek and devote to destruction all that they have. Do not spare them, but kill both man and woman, child and infant, ox and sheep, camel and donkey.'"*

Samuel, one of the early leaders of Israel, is ordering not just war, not just pillage but *genocide* against a neighbouring people! Pretty masculine stuff!

No. 3: Exodus 22:18A *"Do not allow a sorceress to live."*

This command of Moses' has meant death for many an innocent woman accused of 'witchcraft'! Sadly, it's still happening today around the world today.

No. 4: Psalm 137:9 *"Happy is he who repays you for what you have done to us – he who seizes your infants and dashes them against the rocks."*

Unsurprisingly this verse is often omitted in church!

No. 5: Judges 19:25-28 *"So the man took his concubine and sent her outside to them, and they raped her and abused her throughout the night, and at* *dawn they let her go. At daybreak the woman went back to the house where her master was staying, fell down at the door and lay there until daylight. When her master got up in the morning and opened the door of the house and stepped out to continue on his way, there lay his concubine, fallen in the doorway of the house, with her hands on the threshold. He said to her, 'Get up; let's go.' But there was no answer. Then the man put her on his donkey and set out for home."* Group rape of servants is permissible according to the bible! More benefits for men!

No. 6: Romans 1:27 *"In the same way also the men, giving up natural intercourse with women, were consumed with passion for one another. Men committed shameless acts with men and received in their own persons the due penalty for their error."* Homophobia started right there! Were the authors macho men?

No. 7: Judges 11:30-1, 34-35: *"And Jephthah made a vow to the Lord, and said, 'If you will give the Ammonites into my hand, then whoever comes out of the doors of my house to meet me, when I return victorious from the Ammonites, shall be the Lord's, to be offered up by me as a burnt-offering.' Then Jephthah came to his home at Mizpah; and there was his daughter coming out to meet him with timbrels and*

with dancing. She was his only child; he had no son or daughter except her. When he saw her, he tore his clothes, and said, 'Alas, my daughter! You have brought me very low; you have become the cause of great trouble to me. For I have opened my mouth to the Lord, and I cannot take back my vow.'"
The 'Loving Father' wants your daughters burnt for dancing apparently!

No. 8: Genesis 22: *'Take your son, your only son Isaac, whom you love, and go to the land of Moriah, and offer him there as a burnt-offering on one of the mountains that I shall show you.'*
The 'Loving Father' also wants your sons burnt!

No. 9: Ephesians 5:22: *"Wives, submit to your husbands as to the Lord."*
Biblical authorisation of misogyny! Can it have been written by men perchance?

No. 10: 1 Peter 2:18: *"Slaves, submit yourselves to your masters with all respect, not only to the good and gentle but also to the cruel."*
Slavery gets biblical endorsement!

Do you still want to make the Bible your moral compass? Or are you prepared to cherry-pick your way through your 'Holy' book?

Many religious leaders will go into contortions of justification over the many atrocious quotes often using historical context as an explanation. My point is, even if the passages are inappropriate today, the vast majority of the population, who are not academics or Christian apologists, will take them at face value and not bother with the paragraphs of theological interpretation. And, why can't god express herself more clearly, isn't she omnipotent?

Failure of religions to deliver their claims

This is not a new observation – in the third century BC, ancient Greek philosopher, **Epicurus**, said:

> *"Is God willing to prevent evil, but not able?*
> *Then he is not omnipotent.*
> *Is he able, but not willing?*
> *Then he is malevolent.*
> *Is he both able and willing?*
> *Then whence cometh evil?*
> *Is he neither able nor willing?*
> *Then why call him God?"*

Natural Disasters

Terrible things happen too often. In July 2010 floods ravaged Pakistan making 6m homeless. On 13th January 2010 the Haitian earthquake killed 230,000. 26th December 2004 saw a Tsunami strike Thailand. Way back on August 24th, 79AD, volcanic eruption destroyed Pompeii. God not only failed to prevent these events and many others, he didn't even help with the aftermath. *Does he deserve his 'omnipotent loving father' reputation?*

Like Superman, the Christian God is supposed to be up there listening for our cries and swinging into action when we need help. He is, allegedly:

Omnipresent – everywhere – There is no hiding place from God, he is 'within us and without us' – scary!

Omniscient – all knowing – God is eavesdropping on our every word and has magic CCTV watching every action! His database must have expanded in line with the human population!

Omnipotent – all-powerful – he can do anything, supposedly.

These are three fantastic Unique Sales Propositions! *Who wouldn't sign up to an organisation led by such an impressive figure?* Especially as he is supposed to be a good God; imagine the good that could be done by someone wielding those superpowers! Even if he couldn't prevent an unexpected disaster *(and why wouldn't an omnipotent God be able to do that?)*, surely he could help with the rescuing and clearing up afterwards, couldn't he?

Perhaps he is better at providing guarantees before disasters happen? If that was the case, wouldn't Bishops just pray for their Cathedrals to be spared from lightning strikes and save the cost of lightning conductors and insurance? Maybe the insurance companies have got it right – *what is their understanding of an 'Act of God'?* A disaster so unpredictable and severe that they won't cover it!

At the time of writing, we still don't know the final death toll or total cost of the 2011 Japanese earthquake and tsunami disaster or the 2013 Typhoon in the Philippines. In Haiti, survivors have been on the News praising God for sparing them. Strangely, nobody has blamed God for all the deaths. It's a great job where you get all the praise and none of the blame, isn't it! *Is God good at his job?* No! As a 'loving father' he is a complete failure! Perhaps we should 'let him go'; or, maybe he doesn't exist – that would explain things!

Prayer

'Prayer is an invocation or act that seeks to activate a rapport with a deity, an object of worship, or a spiritual entity through deliberate communication'.
(Source: Wikipedia)

How does a prayer differ from a spell? Well, not by much! In both cases someone mutters some words and hopes they will result in his wishes being fulfilled remotely! As if! And neither of them reliably produces the desired outcome. The only difference is prayers always call upon a 'supreme being' to do their bidding whereas spells don't.

Investigations have been performed to check the effectiveness of prayer. In hospital experiments, no convincing evidence has been found to confirm that prayer works any better than the placebo effect. In fact, one study showed a statistical correlation between patients knowing they were being prayed for and *delayed* recovery!

Way back in 1872, Francis Galton conducted a famous statistical experiment to determine whether prayer had a physical effect on the external environment. Galton hypothesized that if prayer was effective, members of the British Royal family would live longer, given that thousands prayed for their well-being every Sunday.

He therefore compared longevity in the British Royal family with that of the general population, and found no difference.

Sadly, 20,000 children will starve to death today. 20,000 died yesterday and 20,000 will die tomorrow. Their prayers and those of their relatives will not be answered. *Is god not listening (not omniscient)? Or is she unable to save them (not omnipotent)? Or is she on holiday (not omnipresent)?*

*Do you imagine god will listen to **your** prayers? Why?*

Oh, you've heard god's voice in your head, have you? How do you know you weren't dreaming or drunk? If it happens regularly, maybe you should go and see a Doctor about it!

Belief in prayer often goes along with belief in the existence of 'souls' and/or 'spirits' which live in the 'hereafter' and can be contacted by 'séances'. None of this has ever been supported by evidence. In fact, you can win a million dollars if you can provide such evidence! Just contact the James Randi Educational Foundation: www.randi.org

What about the good done by religion?

Well, I have challenged many believers to give me examples of a good product or good service that is exclusively provided by religion, i.e. cannot be provided secularly. One example would do. No-one has accepted the challenge, perhaps because they know that all charitable work can be, and is being, also provided by non-believers. Some of the greatest humanitarian acts currently provided are being done by non-believing billionaires Warren Buffet and Bill and Melinda Gates. Their aid comes without coercion into worship – no strings attached!

The only religious 'good' I can think of is the comfort that belief gives to some insecure people. So the balance sheet looks very lopsided – immense historic and daily harm on one pan of the scales with a feather of delusional comfort on the other side. The only benefit is that crumb of comfort afforded to believers and even that's not good because *it is a deception!* Belief in god is a placebo at best.

Some people complain that 'good' inspired by religion does not have to be *exclusively* provided by it. Well, yes it does if it is to be put on the scales as a benefit belonging to religion in the same way that a medicine has to be effective. Others say that there are no benefits exclusively provided by atheism. Well, that's making the mistake of assuming that atheism is a doctrine or field of endeavour. It's not; it's the absence of those things. There is no hierarchical atheistic organisation, no non-believing 'pope'. The other side of the scales is occupied by Science, which most definitely *does* provide benefits so great that mankind has been able to exceed his bodily capabilities in countless directions.

Religions all purport to be peaceful in theory; unfortunately, none of them are in how they are practiced. Since they all claim to have exclusive truth and be the only way to the 'afterlife', that sets each religion (or sect) against all the others and starts them on a quest to convert the entirety of mankind round to their way of thinking. This is divisive and a recipe for disaster. *Do you welcome Muslims into your Christian church without intending to convert them? Do Mormons permit members to leave the faith without a struggle?*

On the other side of the scales is the immense historical (about 9 million people died in the Crusades) and ongoing daily harm done in the name of The 'Lord'. This includes genital mutilation, misogyny, homophobia, child abuse, denial of medication and acts of suicidal terrorism such as '9/11'.

What grieves me is the extent of atrocities that have been done and are still being done in the cause of a 'Lord' who has no evidential backing. This absence of evidence leads me to conclude that, of all the reasons there are for dispute (territory, wealth, resources, poor communication leading to misunderstanding and demonization, etc.) religious differences are the least justifiable. Extrapolating from historic and daily harm to denigrating all faiths may look like a bit of a leap until you include the fact that they are all groundless deceptions.

So, on balance, the world would be a much better place without gods. Since there is no evidence to indicate that any gods exist, there is nothing to lose by abandoning them, and just think of the immense benefit that could result from a useful redeployment of religious assets. Faiths have siphoned off a huge slice of the wealth of societies; imagine how many schools and hospitals we could build instead of churches!

We currently have the real world *and* a layer of religious unreality competing for precious resources. Also, religions predominantly exploit the poor – could you live with your conscience as a priest enjoying a comfortable life off the donations of your starving congregations? *Is it not immoral to stand back and accept or ignore this scourge?*

One of my internet correspondents said, *"Religions provide a source of solace for weak-minded individuals, and I'm not presumptuous to think it's my responsibility to take it away from them."* Well, I'm a teacher, so I *do* accept the challenge of strengthening their minds to help them resist deception. Tobacco offered solace to weak minded individuals but society took it upon itself to save them from the associated damaging side effects; I see religion as similar to tobacco – it causes deaths of believers when they commit suicide bombings and, like secondary smoking, kills others nearby too.

Slipping into faith is all too easy: we must beware because 'spiritual' experiences can be induced by drugs, fever, extreme exercise, oxygen deprivation, hypnotism and a helmet containing strong magnets. The recipient will genuinely believe the experience to have truth and value. Some proselytisers, of course, are charlatans; many of them very rich thanks to the promotion of their 'belief'.

I worry that many good people are giving numerical credibility to the acts of extremists by belonging to the same groupings; *why vote for atrocities?* Some, otherwise good, people even adopt intolerant attitudes, based on 'scriptures', themselves. They teach homophobia and misogyny and other practices to their children and so the problems persist; infant boys still die from unnecessary circumcision even in the USA. *Are you saying we should allow all that to continue?*

Summary

As there's no evidence for any god, you might be excused for thinking that's a good enough reason to throw religion out! *Until there is evidence for the existence of a god shouldn't we regard religions with maximum scepticism and try to save our population, especially our children, from possible deception?*

Religions are divisive; their conviction in their own rectitude and their ambition to convert and expand causes territorial conflict between them. This is particularly regrettable because there is no evidence for the existence of any god. Men have died, and are dying, for a being that is merely *postulated*. Even moderates contribute to this needless division by their continued membership. As Brian Flemming says, "Moderates *enable* the fundamentalists."

Yes, there are other reasons for disagreement and battle but, surely, one less reason would be an improvement wouldn't it? Would we miss a reason based on a belief that is non-evidential? What would you say if the Humpty Dumptians constantly fought the Goldilockians? Stop it? It's Folly?

Religions are dangerous – people die from following the advice of their religious leaders. Believers discontinue their medication, children suffer genital mutilation and soldiers are sent into battle for religious causes and under 'instructions from god' received by their ruler who imagines that 'god' is on his side! Just remember, atheists do not become suicide bombers in the name of *no* god! Yes, there have been terrible atheist tyrants like Stalin, Pol Pot and Mao Tse Tung, but they were not inspired or excused by 'supernaturally' authored scriptures of non-belief.

A Concise List of Reasons to be Against Religion:

1. It's based on the proposition that there is a god – there is no evidence for this. It is therefore no more valid than Tinker Bell stories; a deception.
2. Religion provides no benefits that are not also capable of being provided secularly, without coercion.
3. A very great deal of harm is done by fundamentalists; much of it in the name of The Lord.
4. Even moderate believers support detrimental practices such as circumcision, denial of contraception, denial of blood transfusion and organ transplantation.
5. Religion acts as a brake on life saving developments such as stem cell research.

6. Moderates are complicit in the atrocious behaviour of fundamentalists by supporting the same group – their silence is collusion and they recruit their children.

So, religious affiliation is usually a geographical accident, religious texts are not good moral compasses, many atrocious acts are committed in the name of 'The Lord' who has no evidence demonstrating his existence and charity can be, and is being, provided secularly. Would you recommend joining a religion to your friends?

Maybe doubt is not the voice of Satan testing your faith, but the voice of Reason calling you home! I contend that to ignore the harm done in the name of god, to close our eyes to all the killing, maiming, child abuse, misogyny, homophobia, etc, is immoral.

Another accusation that Theists level at scientists is that Science came out of religion. Well, that's true; a century or two ago the only way anyone could get educated was through a church. There was no secular education available so early scientists came out of religion. I accept that Science grew from religion but, as we grow, we throw away the old clothes we have grown out of and keep the new, better fitting ones. This is the Twenty first century, isn't it about time we all grew out of religion?

Real divisions have to be accommodated by tolerance; unreal ones can be abandoned. There is a very long list of religions that have already been abandoned. Do we miss Zeus?

I view a religion as a wedge. At the thick end we have the well meaning moderates inducting their children and doing charitable acts, while at the thin end (the 'business end' of a wedge) we have the fundamentalists committing their atrocities, but it's all the same wedge. If we stop the input of children, we will stop the output of extremists.

"You're basically killing each other to see who's got the better imaginary friend!"
Richard Jeni

12. LIVING WITHOUT GOD

It's easy! Don't believe it when believers say, 'non-believers are immoral, cold, empty, lonely, futile and unhappy', that's just their insulting propaganda of hatred! Christians' behaviour can be very unchristian at times! In the deep south of the USA, non-believers daren't declare their lack of faith for fear of not being able to get a job or accommodation, or of being spat upon in the street. I even feel it's necessary to use a nom-de-plume (pen-name) for this book to try to avoid damaging the Christian market for my other books!

It's arguable that being a Scientific Realist actually *enhances* one's life experience by improving the understanding of our connection with the universe. *Cannot a watchmaker appreciate the craftsmanship of a watch mechanism more than the owner who simply looks at the watch face on his wrist? Cannot a musician enjoy music better than a non-musician because he can focus on each instrument's part instead of simply hearing an overall sound? Why would knowing more about something detract from its magnificence?* Surely a greater understanding of nature can only improve appreciation and, therefore, life. And another bonus is no 'hell' to fear!

As for the 'meaning of life', *well, does the life of a snail have meaning? What about a goat? Or a daffodil? A tapeworm?* As explained in Chapter 1, searching for meanings is a peculiarity of our highly adapted brains. We are programmed to identify questions and to seek solutions, even where there may be none, for example we see a face on the moon.

The big 'religious' questions mostly begin with 'why'. Science can answer questions that begin with 'how', 'what', 'where', 'when', etc but not 'why'. This is because 'why' is not just a question; it is often also a statement because it contains an implied assumption: that there is a purpose or cause. Who says there must be one? That expectation is just a product of the human brain's evolved 'software': the mind.

To imagine that we are somehow 'special' and are here to follow 'god's' plan' is the height of conceit. *Why would 'he' create a universe about 13.8 billion light years ago specifically for a creature that only arrived about a mere 200,000 years ago?* Surely he needn't have wasted all that time! *And why should we assume that we are his favourites? Isn't that pure egomania?*

The 'purpose' of all creatures is very simple: it's to breed in an attempt to ensure the continuation of their species. Beyond that, you will have to provide 'meaning' for yourself. As a gross generalisation, women often find meaning in having children (my first wife, upon the birth of a baby said, "I know now that I've done what I came for.") and men like to build something – to leave a legacy of some sort.

Want a purpose? Make your own! I recommend study and research; particularly of science. The discovery of information old and, especially, new is very rewarding.
But it isn't all about advantages; there's also the absence of disadvantages. As Bishop John Shelby Spong says, *"The church is in the guilt and control business."* God-fearers are so called because they are taught to be scared of the eternal inferno of 'Hell' and of 'Satan' ('Beelzebub', Lucifer or the 'Devil'). They have to worry about where they might go in the 'afterlife' and what might happen to their 'souls'. Non-believers know that all those things are unlikely to be real so we have none of those terrors.

Given that all societies have their own concept of a god or multiple gods and goddesses; given that religions, like mankind itself, are sexually obsessed (virginity, homophobia, circumcision, celibacy, adultery, etc.); given that religious institutions, like all human groupings, are hierarchical; given that we are supposedly 'made in god's image'; given that all religions claim to provide a highly desirable 'afterlife', etc. *Isn't it highly probably that faiths are a human fabrication?*

Conclusion: We have most likely created god.

Non-believers live normal, happy, lives; they love their children. More importantly, there are no non-believing suicide bombers; we do not kill in the name of *no* god! Just remember, 98% of the criminals in US jails call themselves Christians!

A list of some famous non-believers:
Bill Gates
Warren Buffet
Jeremy Clarkson
Sir Richard Branson
Stephen Fry
Hugh Laurie
Brad Pitt
Joaquin Phoenix
Sir Ian Mckellen
Bob Geldoff KBE
Ricky Gervais
Jodie Foster
Steve Wozniak
And many more unlisted or still in the closet!

When people ask, *"Why do you attack religion so? What's the harm in letting people believe?"* Here's what to say: *"I don't want to live in a world where non-evidential beliefs influence political thought and laws. I don't want my kids to be led up the garden path. I don't want the intolerance to alternative views that causes hatred and violence. I don't want society to have to suffer the acts of religious extremists."*

To those who accuse me of stepping outside my own specialism to take on religion, a subject they like to think I know little about, I say, *"It's you who are stepping on to my turf with your 'explanations' of the origin of the universe and everything in it."*

By now you may be wondering, atheist or agnostic? Which is best? Well, although the etymology of atheism is 'a' = without, 'theos' = god so it should mean living without belief in a personal god, in common usage it gets twisted to mean without a lot of things such as morals, purpose, empathy, warmth, hope, and friendship! I don't want that bundle applied to me! I recognise that people of faith selfishly imagine that they have exclusive access to those things and that they would suffer loss of them if they rescinded their beliefs. This is why I offer Science as the alternative to religion - a proven methodology offering hope and purpose which might fill the 'gap' they fear.

Furthermore, 'atheist' should not be taken to mean there is no god, it means *living* without god, in other words *not worshipping her*. No one can prove there is no god but the absence of evidence might be considered a good reason for choosing to define oneself as an atheist.

We are all born without a faith so we all start life as atheists and, until evidence for the existence of a god is produced, we will all be living 'without god' – we are all atheists! Tell that to your theist friends!

'Atheist' is an unsatisfactory description for another reason: it's an unnecessary word. Theists claim that it is a reaction to believing and therefore it affords belief a sort of justification! They say, "If there wasn't really a god, you wouldn't have to try to deny him!" They have a point, but this is because the word 'atheist' doesn't need to exist. I don't have a bicycle but we haven't found the need to define me as an 'acyclist' have we! If we had to have a special word for all the things that people are *without*, the 'a' section of the dictionary would take up a separate volume! Lack of something is usually a default position not a positive move, unless you have abandoned it like teetotallers or vegetarians.

When I'm giving talks, I sometimes illustrate the foolishness of grouping people on the basis of what they lack by asking the audience how many of them *don't* keep a pet rabbit. I then say, "Right, all of us non-rabbit owners are the 'abunnyists' and we have five minutes to write the scriptures of abunnyism!" Once, a man said, 'Ah, but that's not comparable because you believe in the existence of bunnies'. Well, no I don't. I don't have to. Bunnies are evidential. We can collect data on bunnies by weighing them, taking their temperature, collecting their exhaled CO_2 and in many other ways. *Belief* in bunnies is unnecessary.

Similarly, although the etymology of agnostic is 'a' = without, 'gnostic' = knowledge (in other words, as Sir Patrick Moore was fond of saying, 'we just don't know') in respect to the existence of god, in common usage it is taken to mean 'unknowable'. Well, that is an assumption too far for me! How can we know something is unknowable? Once upon a time, plagues were attributed to an all powerful god's mysterious ways which were assumed to be 'unknowable'. We now know they are due to bacteria transmitted by rats.

'Unknowable' is, for me, pathetically defeatist. My attitude is 'Let's find out!' We simply don't know *yet!* That's why I prefer 'Non-believer' to both 'atheist' and 'agnostic', and it fits in with my understanding that personal beliefs are monumentally unimportant. Since we are ephemeral apes it is vainglorious to imagine that our fickle choices have significance.

IMAGINE

You are newly born. Your eyes don't focus properly yet. You are programmed to be cute so your carers will fall in love with you while you are helpless. You gurgle and cry and soon learn to lock eyes with your carers and to smile fetchingly. You have no hatred. You have no religion.

If your parents happen to be Christian, they are about to fill you up with Christianity. If they are Muslim you will get a dose of Islam. Jewish: Judaism, Hindu: Hinduism. Dear reader, I think you get the picture.

In some cases, your parents will have pieces cut off your genitalia just to show everyone that you belong to their religion. They, and their priests, will teach you that their religion, the one you have been dedicated to, without consultation, after all you can't speak yet, is the only right one and that all other beliefs are wrong.

You may be sent to a single faith school, which will confirm the impression that your religion makes you special, chosen by 'god', and divides you from the rest of society, the 'heathens' or 'infidels'. A few of your peers may become radicalised into fundamentalists who may kill in god's name.

Repeated exposure to rituals in early childhood can result in difficulty escaping from a doctrine at a later stage of life. New research on epigenetics indicates that early experiences can actually alter the expression of genes and this alteration can even be passed down the generations!

Please raise your children in a secular way; if they want to join a religion when they are old enough to make an informed decision, that's up to them.

No child is born religious. Please let them stay that way.

***

One thing is certain, whatever discoveries and technological achievements mankind makes in the future will be made by following Scientific Method, not by theologists or priests re-interpreting ancient religious texts.

CONCLUSIONS

Religion is a divisive, dangerous deception

1. There is no evidence for the existence of any god.
2. Until there is evidence, the sensible default position is scepticism.
3. Much harm has been done and continues to be done by some believers.
4. Charitable acts can be, and are being, done secularly.
5. The idea of a god has no more benefit than a placebo.
6. Most religions have died out over time.
7. The continued existence of 'Faiths' is a failure of Science education.
8. Correcting this failure is a mission worthy of pursuing for the benefit of mankind.

Raison d'être

Why have I written this book? Maybe this conversation on a well-known social media site will explain:

Me: I consider that helping people to see that they are being deceived and fleeced is a virtuous service. Don't you?

Him: That's the same thing Jehovah Witnesses think when they go door to door and annoy us with *their* truth. Where do you draw the line between allowing people to see your alternative and just being a pest?

Me: Possession of evidence is the key. Science has it; JWs don't. Like all religions, theirs is bogus. So, science is better. Besides which, we don't go cold calling!

Him: My question isn't whether what you sell is true or not, my question is, granted *you* believe your evidence points to something but usually, the other person doesn't care. (Fact is, so-called evidence has been disproven time-and-time again when new understanding or theories are tested). So where then do you draw a line between the so-called virtue of your showing them this and simply letting people be free to decide for themselves, even if you perceive theirs as flawed or, in your word, bogus?

Me: I use the word 'bogus' to refer to non-evidential

claims. But I do not believe in science. Science does not require belief. Evidence is not disproved because it was never proved. Evidence is just evidence; it's what scientists base Theories on. Proof is only available to mathematicians. Nothing is ever proven in science, it's only ever assigned a level of probability. And truth is relative not absolute. All scientific knowledge is provisional and open to revision if new evidence arrives. What I am trying to do is educate. If you would prefer the freedom to remain ignorant that is your right. Isn't education virtuous?

Him: And yet 'bogus' has its definition, which is 'fake'.

Re: 'education', that's stretching the definition frankly. Many of the people we speak of are educated, some very educated, and they know as much or more science than you and I. I know a number of these people.

What you're really selling is not science, it's a belief that that science is enough. That it is complete without their beliefs to explain life. Would this not be a line where 'teaching' becomes imposing your way of seeing the world on them?

Like I said, I know some of these people, and no one needs to talk about big bang, evolution or compassion to them, they simply choose to believe in a God above all else too. Just as you and I choose not to, and would frankly not enjoy being approached time and time again by Religious people trying to sell their beliefs to us.

The moment we start to see ours as right, and theirs as definitively wrong, or bogus, and hence requiring us to teach them, we have managed to go full circle to do exactly what they do, that we rebelled against ourselves when younger.

Fact is, I get concerned when people assign the word 'Virtue' to any point of view, religious or not, because then it seems to give it credibility for being imposed or rudely pushed forward, especially in the face of opposing views.

Me: Respect! Yes, some are very educated, a few even in science. It is a conundrum to me that such people can understand the importance of evidence on the one hand and ring fence an area of thought that is non-evidential and immune from scrutiny on the other. I know a science teacher who delivers his evidential subject all week then, on Sunday, flips a switch in his head and goes to church!

How can beliefs explain life, or explain anything, when they are not evidence based? They are placebos at best; self-imposed hoodwinks at worst.

If science is 'not enough', shouldn't we reduce our expectations and become comfortable with a lower level of certainty, not replace it with bogus 'certainty'?

The fact that there is a flag on the moon, put there by the application of science, should be convincing - when did belief achieve anything like that?

Yes, there are some unanswered questions but coming to terms with 'we just don't know' must be preferable to goddunit.

I'll tell you why this is an important mission - it's because Aztecs used to believe it was necessary to kill a man at sunset and hold up his still beating heart, to 'ensure' that the sun rose again next morning. That notion has gone, thankfully, but many religious follies continue to harm mankind.

But I don't 'see my view as right and theirs as wrong'. I don't even see it as *my* view. Science is constructed on discoveries. These are available in the environment for anyone to find. I'm merely pointing in their direction and saying, 'Look at this, isn't it fantastic!' Public domain information cannot be possessed anymore than Livingstone could own Africa despite his ludicrous claims on behalf of Queen Victoria.

Surely, attempting to save humanity from divisive and dangerous deceptions is virtuous, isn't it?

Spookily, the JWs have just been at my door!

AFTERTHOUGHT

'Godbuster', although an eye-catching title, is a bit of a misnomer. I am not against god. How could I be? There is no evidence for her existence. What I am against is *religion: belief and faith*.

When you vote for a political party you give it your support and thereby you share responsibility for what it does to your country when in power. The same endorsement occurs when you belong to a religion; this means that even moderates are culpable for extremists' behaviour. Do you want to support one of the groups that divide mankind into disagreeable factions on the basis of myths?

Hopefully, Godbuster has provided you with information about belief, non-belief and the importance of proper evidence to justify choices. If not, then maybe it has provided you with an assurance that it is okay to doubt. Either way, I hope it has at least caused you to think twice before inducting young children into a faith – that is a decision that should be theirs and should be left to an age when an informed choice can be made.

Belief in a faith can be so hazardous it should be fitted with a child-proof cap!

Some Unholy Questions

1. Did god give us free will?
   Yes?
   How can he have a plan then?
2. Is god in hell?
   No?
   He's not omnipresent then!
3. Is god omniscient?
   Yes?
   Well, if he knows everything, including the future, he can't be omnipotent because he won't be able to change the known things.
4. Is god omnipotent?
   Yes?
   Well, he can't be omniscient then because he can alter what he was supposed to know.
5. Did god make Eve from Adam's rib?
   Yes?
   She had the same DNA then and must have been male! It was Adam and *Steve!*
6. Did god create light on the first day?
   Yes?
   But the sun wasn't created until the fourth day!
7. Did god create plants on day three?
   Yes?
   What powered their photosynthesis on day three then? There was no sun until day four!

Post Script

While I've been writing this book, scientific research has come up with a possible mechanism that may apply to the inheritance of a tendency to believe. Epigenetic studies have revealed that modifications of the expression of the message on DNA (by methylation and acetylation of the bases – the 'rungs' on the helical 'ladder'), which occurs *as a result of experiences during infancy*, can be passed down the generations! The investigations have been done with nervous or calm mice raised in stressful or peaceful environments but I wonder if it might apply to exposure to the rituals of religion, some of them *deliberately traumatic*. Does childhood indoctrination have a *physical* effect on our genome? Does it bring a new pertinence to the expression 'hard-wired'? Does it explain die-hards? Is this why belief runs in families? Might this explain why it is harder to shake off a belief than ordinary memories? Is this why faith is not vulnerable to reason and logic?

Am I trying to combat *science?*

My own subject?

Aaargghhh!

www.ingramcontent.com/pod-product-compliance
Lightning Source LLC
Chambersburg PA
CBHW071954100426
42738CB00043B/2991